Step Back in Time

See

Historic Cataloochee Valley of the Elk

Best Regards
Hattie Davis

Hattie Caldwell Davis
P. O. Box 274
Maggie Valley, NC 28751

Printed in USA
2002

Publisher: Hattie Caldwell Davis

Editor: Opal Ward

Cover: Photo by Fred Weiser, Wildlife Artist, Townsend, Tn.

ISBN 0-9670689-4-0

This book can be ordered by mail. Each book autographed by the author and shipped promptly. For each book $ 19.95 + shipping $3.00(NC Tax only $1.30).
Send check To:
Hattie C. Davis
PO Box 274
Maggie Valley, N.C. 28751

Contents

Chapter Page

1. A Step back in Time Cataloochee Valle In Great Smoky Mountain National Park 7

2. Building the Cataloochee Turnpike 18
   (1) Mr. Richard Neely Barber....................... 34
   (2) Dr. H. Woody... 37
3. Ox Drawn Wagon To California 44

4. Uncle Steve Woody Tells how it was in 1866....... 66
   (1) Dr. Myron Coulter's Speech 70

5. Education and Schools in Cataloochee Township.73
   (1) Address by Dr. Roy Carroll.................... 73
   (2) Memories of Little Cataloochee.......... 83
   (3) Speech by Lamar Gudger - Congressman US House of Representatives............ 91

6. People of Cataloochee descendents...................... 95
   (1) Caldwells marry into 28 different sir names.. 139

7. Buildings in Cataloochee before the Park 160
   (1) Dedication of Cook Cabin 197

8. Cataloochee Furniture.. 223

9. Cataloochee People before and After the Park... 250

10. Stitching Fingers back on.................................. 285

11. Naillon Family 291

12. Nola's Memories... 299

13. History in the Making
Elk/ Panther in Cataloochee 303

14. Short Stories.. 314
(1) Crestmont a Town on Mt. Sterling ... 314
(2) Boogerman Trail.................................... 316
(3) Cemeteries.. 322
(4) Diseases and Remedies........................ 323
(5) White Swelling...................................... 325
(6) Their Spirit Didn't Leave There......... 337
(7) Pearl Throws Hat Away........................ 339
(8) 5 Million Dollar Donation..................... 341

Dedicated to her Memory

This book is dedicated to the memory of my mother, Pearl Valentine Caldwell. She was born in Tennessee. Then moved to Little Cataloochee with her mother, Grandma Emma Killian Valentine about 1920 when Emma's daughter-in-law, Loretta Messer Valentine, became very ill with influenza and died in childbirth. Grandma Emma took her daughters Pearl and Ressie to take care of the premature baby, 2½ lbs and they were able to raise her. (See the story in *Reflections of Cataloochee Valley Page 40.)*

In 1923 Pearl became the bride of Eldridge Caldwell in Big Cataloochee. Their four children were born there, Nell, Hattie, Helen and Ken. The first born, Nell, died when she was five years old, Mother never got over the hurt she felt and many times in her life she talked about it, she lived to be 91 years of age, and talked more about Nell in her last years than before.

In 1934 when the GSMN Park acquired all the property in the Cataloochee Township, all the people had to leave. We moved to Maggie Valley on Campbell Creek where Mother and Daddy spent the rest of their life.

Mother was probably the last of the "Pony Express" mail carriers she died in 1995. As a young lady of eighteen she was a substitute mail carrier from Little Cataloochee on horseback. Mercus Hall, a neighbor got the contract to carry the mail, but he often had to go check on his cattle, off on some mountain top or work on the farm.

Mother liked to ride horses and was not afraid to ride the five miles through the woods to the Nellie Post Office in Big Cataloochee, except one place which was overgrown with big trees, making it dark as night. She said sometimes it sounded like people talking but no one was there. But she was riding "Little Mag" her favorite horse, and she carried her rider very fast through that spot. She said all along the way there were logs and fallen trees. She said her little horse could just sail over those logs as pretty as you please. Finally someone told her the water flowing underneath some loose rocks down deep in the ground caused the sound of voices.

Mother took a big part in the church and when we moved to Maggie Valley, the Methodist Church was old and in bad shape due to the great depression.

Eventually another church was started; there was not enough money to pay for it. The women decided to have church dinners to make money to help pay on the church. Mother was in the group of women that cooked; she made wonderful homemade rolls and was a really good cook. Those women cooked many meals.

Finally the mortgage was paid off.

Maggie United Methodist Church

Maggie Valley, N. C.

The church was a beautiful little church with a bell tower and with a beautiful steeple pointing to

Heaven. (Now the Maggie Methodist Church has been enlarged and some changes made).

Mother was a good seamstress. She made all our clothes until we were in high school. She could do beautiful needlework, crochet, embroidery, appliqué, cross-stitch, smocking and other kinds of needlework. She was very artistic and made many beautiful crafts. She grew beautiful flowers and nice big gardens, canned and preserved lots of food.

She spent much of her life helping and taking care of the sick, her child Nell who died, Grandma Caldwell, her sister Aunt Mae Miller and daddy and her mother, grandma Valentine with some help from her sisters with her.

Mother was a very strong disciplinary, us kids couldn't get away with any mischief, she intended for us to grow into responsible honorable adults.

In addition, this book is dedicated to my sons Gil and Don Grasty, all of my grand children and great grand children.

Introduction

This is really a continuation of *"Reflections of Cataloochee Valley and its Vanished people in the Great Smoky Mountains."* Some years ago when I was doing research, I could see those dear old Cataloochee folks would soon be gone, so I collected as much information as I possibly could, I knew the history would soon die with those who had lived it. As a result I got much more information than I could get into one book. I will try not to repeat too much, I will just refer to *"Reflections of Cataloochee"* where the stories are interconnected.

As early as 1790's settlements were established in the Haywood area. The county was organized from the western portion of Buncombe County in 1808, with Waynesville as the county seat. But owing to the extreme topography, Cataloochee was the last part of Haywood to be populated by white people. During the 1820's grassy balds near Bunk Mountain, the Balsams, the Ledge and other places were used as summer cattle pasture grounds by settlers living in other parts of Haywood. Drovers and hunters built the first structures in the area. The Cataloochee area is located in the northwestern portion of Haywood County, and it is characterized by mountain slopes that rapidly rise from an elevation of 3,000 feet to over 6,000 feet. In the valleys along the creek was rich virgin soil, good for farming but oh what rough hard work to clear it in the beginning (1834-1934 see *"Reflections of Cataloochee"* 304 pages)

For one hundred years these three small communities of unusual historic interest lay nestled in the Great Smoky Mountains of Western North Carolina. Isolated from other populated areas by rugged mountain terrain, the families of Cataloochee formed a close-knit interdependent group. The families relied upon one another to live and worked to help each other and finally they had much cleared land to farm, large herds of livestock, nice homes, plenty of fine timber and they were happy, never dreaming they would have to give it up, in the 1930's the descendants of the areas pioneer families were evicted to make way for the Great Smoky Mountains National Park

Chapter 1

A Step Back in Time -- Cataloochee Valley In the Great Smoky Mountain National Park

Yes it is a place where you can step back in time. The buildings are about a hundred years old and some are well over a hundred years. It is a place so lovely you are struck by all of nature's beauty, peace and tranquility and for a short time you feel the freedom that our ancestors knew. You can visit our little white church with its original handmade pews and pulpit, imagine the big pot bellied wood stove which sat in the center of the church and little kerosene lamps with bright reflectors hanging on the wall between each window. And a larger oil lamp, which sat on the pulpit to provide light for the minister to read for night services.

You can go out and walk by the creek flowing gently along, breathe the pure cool air of a gentle breeze, seems like sometimes it carries faint notes of *Amazing Grace, In the Sweet Bye and Bye* or some other hymn that has been sung in that little church for more than a hundred years. You can envision years gone by when there were wagonloads of people coming to church and some came in buggies, on horseback or walking. Imagine the wagons, horses and buggies under the trees, which the people came to church in. As you walk along these lush woodlands and nature trails it brightens your day. When life's constant pressure start to take their toll you can seek refuge in this beautiful place.

You can unwind in the solitude and you are in another world, some call it Paradise.

As you come to the little schoolhouse built 1906 you see how plain it is, bare planks floors and walls, the little wooden desks. Once it was heated by a big potbellied stove. I think I smell the old chalk used on the black board, I go stand by the beautiful clear creek and sometimes I think I hear faint echoes of children at play. Even though it was a plain little country school, there was a foundation laid that gave students the confidence to accomplish all they could in life. In another chapter, you will read of some who were born in Cataloochee and started school there in the plain little school then went on to become professionals and business men and successful farmers. The small school in Little Cataloochee laid the same foundation.

As you go on up the road you can see the big fields where once there were perfect straight rows of corn or maybe a big hay field. Now you may see elk roaming in the meadows where once our cattle, horses and sheep were grazing prior to the Park.

As I look back about seventy years ago and remember the way it was on Sunday afternoon after church lots of people came to visit at our house

(Caldwell house). The yard was full of people, grown ups pitching horseshoes. There were all sizes and ages playing baseball, and lots of people on the front porch talking. Of course the women of the house were busy in the kitchen preparing dinner (as we called our midday meal). There were children on the grapevine swings at the edge of the woods, and little girls making playhouses and boys playing in the branch, catching lizards and tadpoles to put on the girls.

Soon we could smell the delicious food wafting in the air, we knew it would soon be time to eat. On Sunday we always had a white damask tablecloth and flowers on the table when they were in bloom.

What a feast we had, usually a big platter of ham from our smokehouse, hot biscuits, fried apples, a big pot of chicken and dumplings, all kinds of fresh vegetables from our garden, a big strawberry or blackberry cobbler, plenty of good whole milk and good home made butter. We often had a large platter of fried fish. Always so much good home grown food, nothing much was bought except sugar, coffee, salt, flour and a few spices, they grew several herbs for medicine and some for adding flavor to the food. Oh, how I would like to sit at that table again. You can see it and the peg leg bench at the Shelton House, Waynesville, N.C.

On Sundays we had so many visitors that the table was set two or three times. After the big meal was over the games started again and daddy (Eldridge) would cut the men and boys hair, he never charged a cent.

Now on Monday morning it was a far different story, nobody was playing and everyone was working.

The women had a big fire under a large black kettle, heating water to wash the clothes. When the water was hot it was dipped up and poured into washtubs. Then the washboard and lye soap were used to scrub the clothes, then they were boiled in the big kettle with lye soap then rinsed and hung on the line to dry. How fresh and clean the clothes smelled. Of course there was starching and ironing to do - with flat irons which were heated by the fire in the fireplace or on the cook stove. It took most all day to do the laundry; they had to take time out to cook the midday meal. Ironing was an all day job usually done on Tuesday.

The men would be plowing in the fields, children hoeing corn or what ever crop they were working in. Most of the visiting was done on Sunday because there was plenty of work the rest of the week, but they would always stop their work if a neighbor was sick or needed help.

Nothing much had changed, time has stood still in Cataloochee from 1934 until Feb. 2, 2001 when the Park Service brought in 25 elk. The elk are drawing large crowds, Cataloochee is not the quiet peaceful place of solitude that it was, but the elk are beautiful and the valley and creeks and all of nature is at your fingertips, enjoy.

Judge Alley: *Random Thoughts and Musings of a Mountaineer.*

It inspires in my heart a reverence so profound, its ruggedness and vastness, its matchless splendor and its lavishness of beauty sink into my soul and leaves my spirit straining at its earthly bounds to gaze with longing eyes toward the Infinite Power which ordered its existence.

This is exactly how most of us feel about Cataloochee and all of our mountains.

Whiskey

Usually those who did make whiskey were those who came in late, after all the best land was taken and they could only get a scrap of rough mountain land, growing corn and making whiskey was the only way to get a dollar to support their family, even though he may get caught and go to jail, he would risk it before letting his children go hungry. They had finer principals than some of the men today who leave their wife and children to be supported by welfare.

There are a few poor and unfortunate people, like you will find everywhere, but those outside writers portrayed all mountain people the same.

People outside our mountains had not been educated about what fine upstanding people the mountaineers were. Judge Alley wrote: "They show pictures of dilapidated log cabins, saying it is the typical home of the typical mountaineer, which is misleading and has no basis for fact. They make no mention of the beautiful homes, fine schools, imposing churches. They do not speak of the distinguished mountain men. They like to write of poverty, want, ignorance, dissolution and distress of the mountain people.[1]

---

[1] Judge Felix Alley "*Random Thoughts and Musings of a Mountaineer*" 1941 p. 217.

A lot has changed in the more than fifty years since Judge Alley wrote that book in 1941, then most of the outside writers made fun of us, saying it's the land of make do or do without. Now they say "Oh, what fine artist and craftsmen those mountain people are", the fine furniture they build, beautiful carvings and all the beautiful handcrafted items they can make, the beautiful baskets, and pottery and fine needle work and weavers and those beautiful hand made quilted quilts.

Now people come here and pay big prices for these items, many come here to learn some craft, others bring their crafts here to sell and some come to teach a different craft.

Weaving and dying was a real art then and now it is taught in many places.

The carding of cleaned washed sheep's wool into rolls and from there to the spinning wheel, where it was spun into thread of desired size, uniformity and smoothness were the first processes. Then the thread was ready for the loom.

It required deft hands, experience and a proper sense of coordination for anyone to become a skilled weaver. It took nothing less than a brilliant mind to weave coverlets of intricate design.

Just as it took skill to make the loom, there were many in the old days who were qualified as skilled weavers, perhaps your great grandmother or other relative.

Granny Pap (Mary Ann Naillion Colwell) was an excellent weaver of coverlets she taught her daughters to weave those beautiful coverlets, they were Harriett Colwell Cook, Matilda Colwell Bennett and Nancy Jane Colwell Palmer.

Dying Yarn

Dying the yarn and woven cloth was quite an art within its self; it required skill because there were no ready- made-store bought dyes. Indigo blue and copas were perhaps the principal dyes used, however a brown dye solution was obtained by boiling walnut hulls, pokeberry for rose and other plants were used for different colors. Weaving was carried on here to a great extent, even as early as 1810, according to Mr. W.C. Medford - *Early History of Haywood County*.

Perhaps the only craft that was truly appreciated by the outsiders in the early days, was the weaving of the beautiful coverlets of such intricate designs, and the fine wool cloth they wove, also a cloth called woolsey-linsey, made from flax (they grew) and wool from their sheep's backs. The flax was a fibrous plant that could be woven into linen cloth.

Some lady came to this area, she saw the fine weaving and was amazed that nearly all the women folks here knew how and a large percent of them had looms. She was so impressed how they could follow the complicated patterns (called drafts) she knew these women had to have fine clear minds. She was also impressed with the smooth fine wool cloth and woolsey-linsey they wove. She got a school started in Asheville and started a business called, Biltmore Homespun it was a very successful business and the material and the suits made from it are very fine.

Cataloochee the Way it Was

This story of Cataloochee is a story of one of the last frontiers of Eastern America, where there is snuggled deep within the Great Smoky Mountains, a beautiful place where time seemed to be measured in eons and the tick of a clock was seldom heard.

You would have traveled there on a rough narrow steep crooked gravel road, you climb to the top of Cove Creek Gap, the elevation of about 4600 ft. then you are at the border of the Great Smoky Mountains National Park, from there you descend to the floor of the valley. The past seems to slip away gradually and before you know it you are face to face with the stern reality of another world. Where four generations of hardy pioneers had managed to get here first by a rough cut out cattle trail. They came with a pack horse or an oxen with very few articles, a rifle, a bedroll, a few cooking vessels and their Bible, they cleared the land built log cabins, farmed and raised large families, made their living raising cattle, hogs, sheep, and other livestock.

The high mountain ranges surround this beautiful valley, separating Cataloochee from the rest of the world; you would have been far away from the hustle and bustle of the world. The hush and quite of the peaceful beautiful valley is so inspiring, it was like heaven's little annex.

You would forget the speeding cars, buses, trucks and the noise that you left behind in another world. The hush and quite of the peaceful beautiful valley would overcome you and you realize that God made this place special.

You could have walked along the edge of Cataloochee Creek and have seen the large fields where rock walls and split rail fences guarded the crops and men working. You could have seen the barns and lots of out buildings, haystacks, beautiful well-built log cabins, old corn mills, post office and general store, large homes and children playing in the yards, fields and creeks, lots of cattle, sheep, hogs, horses, chickens, ducks and geese and maybe other animals. All of this attest to the living proof of those men and women who conquered a wilderness. They asked nothing of the wilderness but a chance to go their way, to rear their children, to live in peace and happiness. They were friendly and extended their hospitality to all who came along.

Chapter 2

CATALOOCHEE TURNPIKE

The Cataloochee Turnpike

CATALOOCHEE TURNPIKE

This whole article was supposed to be in *"Reflections of Cataloochee Valley"* but it was condensed due to space. When you read this chapter you should understand why most of the Cataloochee descendants want to keep that historic road, due to the blood sweat and tears and even death by their ancestors to get the road built.

In 1825 a rough narrow cattle road had been blazed (cut out) and made sufficient for a stock drovers road. A few Jonathan Creek Citizens did it, Joshua Allison I. being one of the leaders in the movement. However the road was authorized by the county court. It led from the right hand prong of Cove Creek, above the Davis place (where the toll gate was.) to the Cataloochee Creek, and was called "Cataloochee turnpike". Allison was made keeper of the tollgate. He was to have the gate fees as his for keeping said road in good repair and etc. There were the stated fees. Allison was to collect.

For a man and a horse 18¾ cents, for an extra pack horse 6½ cents, for each head of hogs 1 cent each, for cattle two cents per head.

No fees for vehicles were mentioned what so ever, because we suppose it was entirely impossible for such, except possibly a half sled maybe. Mostly oxen, packhorses or mules were used to get supplies in. Note we must not get this first old cattle road into Cataloochee confused with the much later and remarkable Turnpike, which was finished in 1860.

Mr. H.C. Medford - *Early History of Haywood County*. P. 81.

The people who came into Cataloochee before 1860 had to travel by way of the old rough cut out cattle road for thirty-five years before the Cataloochee Turnpike was built. It was improved in the 20s but it was still rough. Now it is <u>much</u> improved by the Park.

Mr. H.C. Wilburn who was a surveyor for the Park Service wrote about the road, he had a great interest in history and collected quite a lot of valuable information in the late 20's. December 8, 1937 he wrote to Mr. Ned J. Burns, chief of Eastern Museum Division in Washington, D.C. also sent a copy to Superintendent Eakin and Park Naturalist. Mr. Wilburn wrote: Considerable time has been given to investigation of the old Indian Gap Trail, which was later developed and used by white settlers. This trail is historically important. It was used as an ancient Indian Trail; then as a passage across the Smokies by the pioneer settlers in the adjacent areas as a commercial route for the driving of livestock, hogs, mules, and horses between the grazing lands of Tennessee and Kentucky and the cotton growing areas of South Carolina. Federal forces and Confederates also used it during the War Between the States. A map is being prepared that will show the location of the old trail, the points where historical episodes have transpired, and the location of early settlements that were made along this commercial route. Considerable work remains to be done in collecting date, checking records and traditions. This work will be continued and a map furnished when nearly enough complete (may possibly be found in the Park archives or at WCU Cullowhee in the archives). I have always been told that the road (Cataloochee Turnpike) that you travel today mostly follows the old trail Mr. Wilburn wrote about.

In 1810 Methodist Bishop Asbury traveled to Cataloochee to preach to who ever he could find there. We have no record of anyone living there at that time except in the summer time, some who had cattle on the grassy balds grazing until cold weather. They built some kind of camp or temporary place to stay while looking about the cattle. There were some who camped over there to hunt, fish and trap for fur.

Bishop Asbury probably found a few people there, but he wrote in his journal complaining bitterly about the rough terrain. He and his party got lost in overgrown thickets of laurel when they were traveling on the trail.

The Improved Cataloochee Turnpike

The pioneers of this county had to make out with wilderness roads that were worse than logging roads today.

We see the state and county spending millions of dollars today grading great thoroughfares - boring through the mountains, spanning streams with great bridges, and laying the wide, finished ribbons of concrete and asphalt in every direction.

Now for a change in picture let's look back a hundred and fifty years and see the old settlers in this country "mark out" and make a wagon road. (That was the term they used then) These old pioneers in coming here had somehow, already gotten their few belongings through the wilderness to their new homes. (They had generally built log cabins as soon as possible after getting here).

Now the problem was to get the roads cut out and made passable (at least in dry weather) so they could get to the county seat, bring in supplies, get to mill etc. This work was partly at county expense, with the communities furnishing the "hands" or free labor.

The specification for a common wagon road was for it to be ten to twelve ft. wide. This meant such country roads were partly one way, being wider places made at intervals for wagons to pass. But if two wagons met in a narrow place, it would be impossible to pass and too far and steep to back up to one of the wagons to a wide place. The men would unload one wagon then take it apart and lay the load and wagon parts up on the bank, then one wagon could go past and the men would reassemble the other wagon and load it up, then each man went on their way.

"Main Public Roads" "State Roads" and "Toll Roads" were wider, they having various specifications. Before churches and schools, before courthouse and jail before everything except a place of dwelling - roads came first in the county, which was created out of Buncombe County.

The extension of settlements by this time (1809-10) into the woodlands, along the creeks and rivers, back into the coves was getting far ahead of the ability of the county to connect them up with roads. However the county was new making the orders for them. Just how long these folks would have to wait on the roads was uncertain.

These wilderness roads would have been hard to make even with road making equipment, and this was the era of the bull-tongue plow, pick, shovel, Maddox and sledge hamper, prize (pry) pole, "raw-hiding" - and "main strength" and awkwardness in road building. It was cut and slash, drag, push and pull, heave, huff and holler, beat and break sweat and swear!

After chopping and swearing and clearing the right-of-way most of the stumps would be grubbed and dug around, then prized (pried) out. Some would be cut off close to the ground as possible and left in the road. Much draining had to be done, so log culverts (hollow logs) were used. The heavy growth along the forest roads kept many muddy places from drying out, and little could be done about it. Also the narrow-rimmed wagon and cartwheels tended to cut out deep ruts. But, fortunately whenever wagons became mired up, as was often the case "prize poles" were usually kept lying along the road banks of such miry places. Sometimes they would work for hours trying to get out - prying at the mired wheels, putting rocks and timbers etc. under the wheels. Often the extra team would be required to pull it out.

Life under such unfavorable conditions needed the necessary morale to meet them and the fortitude to carry on. These hardy pioneers of this county (and others) most certainly had it. Home life, though generally hard and strenuous also had its pleasantries and social functions told in more detail in other chapters in *"Reflections of Cataloochee"*

After the route had been decided to build a better "Cataloochee Turnpike" Thomas Welch of Cherokee was ordered to begin the survey at first designated this was to begin "at a point near Boyd's on Jonathan Creek" (the Robert Boyd Place) and continue to the "Tennessee Line". Except in a few places the road today practically follows this old survey. Up Cove Creek Mountain and through the gap, at more than 4,500 feet altitude, it went then from Cove Creek Gap making a "thousand turns" to Cataloochee Creek. Thence down this creek, and the road is soon turning after crossing Little Cataloochee in the direction of Mt. Sterling Gap, over 6,000 ft. This gap is reached after again making so many turns that you could get dizzy. Winding down from the gap to Big Creek more turns on the Tennessee line.

Surveyor Thomas Welch of Cherokee reported to the company that he made this survey with a grade of one foot in fourteen, with the exception of a short distance on the Jonathan Creek side of Cove Creek Mountain. From Cataloochee Creek through the Gap of Mt. Sterling to the Tennessee line was made with grade of one foot in twelve.

More over this old surveyor with nothing but an old-fashioned surveyors compass and chain, and probably two or three helpers. He had only three weeks to make his survey and bring in a report. It seems unbelievable, but that is the record.

The road was to be made fourteen ft. wide, but specifications were that on sharp turns the road is to be made eighteen feet wide, so that wagons could take the turns with ease.

The contracts are let with approximately $22,000 in stock was taken by public subscriptions, including $5,000 taken by the state. There being more than 100 individuals subscribers, so finally on December 3, 1855 the road was ready to be let.

Contracts were let in sections of one-half mile each to the lowest bidders. A contractor could take more than one section. It is said there were about 30 to 35 individual contractors for the road. The contracts ran all the way from $30.50 up to $500. William Ramsey bid off the Big Creek bridge January 1, 1858 for $139. (The same year that Levi built his second and larger house in Big Cataloochee, also the same year that Julia C. Palmer gave land for the church/school in Big Cataloochee).

To better visualize the bigness of this undertaking we must remember that these 28 miles of grade traversed some of the wildest and most rugged terrain in Western North Carolina, all covered with dense growths of the forest primeval. Felling trees and clearing out the right-of-way was the first work to be done. Imagine those crews working, stretched out at intervals of a half-mile or more, along the entire distance of 28 miles all at work!

Axes ringing, saws a-singing, hammers swinging - all hands bringing every effort to bear upon the work of getting the road made.

But there are many interruptions, delays and lay-offs. Severe winter weather, stopping work to make crops, and lay-offs for lack of funds was some of them. For grading work they had little more than the ordinary farm implements of that day - picks, mattocks, shovels, small plows, sledge hammers, etc. They didn't even have blasting powder. Instead, they heated the big rocks that couldn't be moved. They pecked on the rocks with iron rods made small holes, then built fires on them; then they had to go down to creek, get water, climb back up the mountain then shattered the rocks by pouring the icy cold water on them, then use a sledge hammers to break the large pieces down to move them. In grading around mountainsides, they would often construct log or rock retaining walls on the lower side of the road in very sloping places, then fill in with dirt, rocks etc.

Finally in spite of all these handicaps, the Cataloochee Turnpike was finished late in October 1860. It had been five years under construction, and twelve years since promotion of it was started.

Every able bodied man was ordered to work on the road six days a year to keep it passable. George Palmer was working on the road one day just before it was completed, he fell dead of a heart attack. He never got to travel the full length of it.

It was unfortunate that the road was completed just before the Civil War, because Col. Kirk and his 600 men came from Tennessee into Cataloochee on this road, stealing, killing, plundering and all other mean things they did. It was the only road across the Smokies.

To read more about Kirks raid on Cataloochee see *"Reflections of Cataloochee"*.

The road was built by stockholders who had an idea of capitalizing on the livestock being driven at the time from East Tennesseeans driving through to South Carolina and Augusta, Georgia markets. All the cattlemen using the grassy balds for pasture in summer and driving their cattle back over the road in the fall and all the Cataloocheeans who used it. The road was opened as a toll road, but as such it wasn't profitable. After twenty years of operation, the toll was discontinued (there was no charge to use it.)

There was a road overseer, he would notify all men subject to road duty in their section to report with hoe, shovel, mattock, pick or an axe, to work on certain sections of the road. Poll tax was $2.00 and the men subject to poll tax, were allowed to work it out on the road, at one dollar per day. The number of days a road hand had to work each year was determined by the overseers as they saw fit, according to bad weather, hard rain, freezes or washouts, would mean more days to work on their road.

The law generally read: all able-bodied male citizens ages 21 to 50 years old. It was an antiquated system but it was in force for one hundred years in this county. The narrow wagon wheels cut deep ruts in the wet weather. The large herds of cattle sheep, hogs and turkeys turned the road into a muddy mess. There were rocks and stumps in the center of the road, but the high wheels of the wagons and buggies could go over them.

Second Improvement of the Cataloochee Turnpike

Finally in the 20's the Cataloochee people voted bonds to modernize the Turnpike. They were to pay part of the cost, but since the lumber companies owned or leased the biggest portion of the mountain land, they would pay the largest amount of money to get the road in better condition.

All agreed to hire Will Medford as the contractor, because he had dynamite! He could get rid of the huge boulders and rock cliffs that were so large they could not be moved by manual labor, in the period between 1855 to 1860 when many Cataloochee men and others were working so hard to build the road, so well described by Mr. Clark Medford: *Early History of Haywood Co.* But try as they may it was impossible to remove the largest rocks sticking out where the road bed should be, they had to make the road go down the hill under the rock then back up, to get the road on grade as surveyed. This was the only way to bypass the rock cliff. Sometimes this detour would be awfully steep but the men being expert horsemen, they knew how to get their wagons through this kind of road. Everyone was glad to get the rocks dynamited out of their way.

You may wonder how a heavy loaded wagon could go down the steep mountain and not run over the horses. The wagons had brakes, which was a big block of wood fastened on to a long wooden handle, one man drove and one pushed forward on the long wooden handle which caused the big block of wood to press back against the back wheel. This took a strong man applying great pressure to slow the wagon, but this would not hold the wagon back if the load was real heavy and the grade was steep.

Gudger and others have told how they would cut a good-sized tree and fasten it to the back of the wagon.

The weight of the tree would help hold back the weight of the heavily loaded wagon, of course when they started uphill, the tree would be cut loose.

Gudger Palmer remembered the Bennett turn was very steep, because of a large rock protruding out of the bank, and they had to travel down under the rock and then back up, this made an awful steep switchback.

The Cataloochee Turnpike is probably the oldest and most historic road in this area. Let us all hope and pray, that it can be kept as it is now, so our young folks and future generations will be able to appreciate all the hard backbreaking work that our ancestors did.

Can you imagine riding on one of the heavy loaded wagons, riding in a buggy, horseback riding or even walking out of Cataloochee? If we can keep the road as is, it will be great contribution to understanding cultural and historic value of the area and the people who lived there. So much as been destroyed we need to keep this road. If a new road is built, it will destroy the old historic road then there will be the long wide ribbons of cement and the mountains cut down, just like all other roads. This Cataloochee Turnpike is truly unique; please help us keep it to preserve its historic value. It has been widen and much improved since the Park took over.

Judge Alley

These men and women had a quality of courage and self-reliance has never before nor since been surpassed. They did not talk of their heroic deeds as exceptional or infrequent, for they were common everyday doings of men and women of that period. Only now, judged by the sheltered standards of our present civilization, can we adequately appreciate the scope and magnitude of their courage, fortitude, and patriotism and today we salute those noble men and women.[1]

Photo: GSMNP

Crews of local men, who paid their poll tax each year with their labor, did roadwork. Wagons were common, but sleds were more common. They were easy to build: you started with two bent sourwood runners and went from there. There seemed to be one for every purpose: Tobacco, hay, logging and general hauling. Sleds were cheap and went where wagons wouldn't go.

---

[1] Judge Felix Alley, *Random Thoughts and Musings of a Mountaineer.*

This is the Cataloochee road today. Those who lived there never had it so good. It has been much improved; it is still steep and full of turns mostly on the same roadbed as the old turnpike.

Barn from the north...

Date: 11/29/1937

Photographer: C. S. Grossman

Homer Caldwell Barn CA-23 Shanty Branch
Cataloochee, NC File No. III-B-10,016
Neg. No. 10,016

This *is how the old roads looked 1937 in dry weather, and much worse in the early years.*

Can you imagine how deep the mud was in wet weather, and the narrow steel rimed wheels of heavily loaded wagons cutting the road deeper and deeper.

Mr. Richard Neely Barber

Mr. Richard Neely Barber was 4 years old when his father built the house on Russ Ave. Waynesville. They had a phone, the number was 27 it was the furthermost north of any phone on Dellwood Road. There was not another phone in the area for many years.

In a letter (8 pages) I received from Mr. Barber, he wrote, our phone served a purpose for at least 20+ years. People from Jonathan Creek, Fines Creek, Cataloochee, Maggie Valley, even Big Creek and Little Cataloochee, when they were desperate for a doctor night and day, they came on horseback, walking or in buggies. The doctors lived over a mile apart in Waynesville.

I knew the people of Cataloochee from time I was five years old, my father took me fishing there often.

I made my first trip to camp and fish in a T-model Ford, no windshield, no top or seats except boards. I paid $25.00 for it, no driver's license required and no licenses plate. Kance McElory was with me that was 1918 or 1919.

The road was the same one in which cattle, sheep, hogs and horses had traveled but practically no cars. We did not see one or hear of anyone owning one. We met many people walking, fishing or riding horses.

The road below the Bennett curve was filled with running water in the road, but not enough to give much trouble. All cars we heard of were said to require at least four people to push and have a value on gas tank to be pumped to give pressure to gas on gravity fed line from gas tank to motor as the road was too steep for gas to feed by gravity.

He wrote, I have been back every year since and have camped about every place one could lay down in and have spent the night in nearly every other house over there.

One Sunday my friend Jim Wooten and I went to visit Mr. Barber, he was very pleased and talked of his trips to Cataloochee. He told of one trip when they run out of gas on the mountain, they had a gallon of kerosene for camping and wondered if it would make the car go, then a man came walking, carrying four half gallon jars of moonshine in a tow sack. We bought a gallon of it and mixed it with the kerosene and poured it into the old car, he laughed and said well the old car didn't know what happened to it, when we cranked it, it spurted and jumped and jerked but she ran and jerked most of the way there.

Mr. Barber had written to me March 11, 1998 in regards to the first Cataloochee book (*Reflections of Catloochee Valley and its Vanished People* same copy as hard back). He wrote that he knew of the book but didn't buy one because he had spent so much time there and had read about Cataloochee, he did not think my book would tell him anything that he didn't already know. But his dear friend (for 65 years) Hugh Rogers gave him a copy. He said he read it from cover to cover, nearly every page brought memories of names and places. Half the names brought memories of places and things some funny, some sad, some happy and many never to be forgotten.

He wrote I would cherish the opportunity of meeting you, I would be most happy for you to pay me a visit and sit a spell. Don't hesitate to drop by I like to feel like I am a friend and neighbor to all in Haywood County.

We had a wonderful visit with Mr. Barber and spent the whole afternoon with him, then saw him at the Cataloochee reunions after that.

Mr. Barber is an expert at growing roses, he brings hundreds of them to both Big Cataloochee and Little Cataloochee reunions, and they are used on the tables, in the church and put on graves. Mr. Barber had so much fun fishing in the Cataloochee Creeks in his young years, now he comes to visit his old friends and brings beautiful roses for the tables and the church windows.

Since this was written, Mr. Barber passed away this year 2002 but his grandson Jeff Henderson brought the roses in honor of his grandfather. When the church bell tolled 29 times and a Cataloochee names were called then Mr. Barber's name was called and the church bell rang again in honor of him, he was a friend to all.

Cataloochee Homecoming

Dr. H. Woody 1950
History Professor at Duke

An unconscious effort to recapture one's strength at natures breast, has kept with us the family reunion or community "homecoming". It is one way in which we can "go back" not as a prodigal, probably sick of fatted calves already, or the local boy who made good, but in response to the elemental longings of one's nature. The trouble with homecoming is that the stark reality of things as they are compared with what they seemed in the long ago is disillusioning. Particularly so, if one notes deterioration and hears it called progress.

This return to Cataloochee is something of a pilgrimage. We want to tread the familiar paths, to look on the simple white tombstones, of our ancestors, to gaze on the friendly, eternal mountains, now disfigured by the gaunt arms of the chestnut trees, to smell the woods and the wild flowers, and to listen to the low monotone of the near-by creek, which lulled us to sleep in the nights of our youth. But this nostalgia, this remembrance of the old home place, the little adventures that cluster in our thoughts - this must give way to the reality of a desolate countryside, houses and barns empty and forsaken, the visible sigh of a dead community. It may be thought that this isolated community without benefit of electricity, movies, telephones, automobiles, no one on Little Cataloochee ever owned an automobile and a buggy was a rarity, (at least not when Dr. Woody was growing up there, he was born 1903. But a few owned vehicles in late 20's or early 30's). But the Cataloochee scene was not so dismal as may be imagined, not nearly so dismal as it has become since the creation of the Park. Their common sense and native skill developed from youth generated a triumph of fact over theory. The poetry in their souls found expression in the old English ballads or the Psalms of the Bible. Needless to say "good living" was the rule. Fish in the creek, honey in the hive, milk in the springhouse, meat in the smokehouse and an apple house stored with a variety of canned vegetables and fresh apples was the accepted order of nature.

In season it was no trouble to pick off a mess of squirrels in early morning or late afternoon. I note for the uninitiated that a young groundhog caught in the early summer, when he was fat on young beans the like, and properly prepared was a delicacy worthy of discriminating people. In such a land poverty could not be widespread. Few indeed were desperately poor.

This life on Cataloochee was very real to me. I spent many summers with Uncle Tine and Aunt Laura; they had a farm of some two hundred acres. Perhaps a third of it was in timber. Some of the remainder was too steep for farm implements more complex than a one-horse plow. A sled was usually more useful than a wagon. The axe, the scythe, the cradle and the grindstone were familiar enough. I remember the hewn log house, consisting of kitchen "big house" and middle room. It was weather boarded from timber sawed on the place. Shingles and boards for the roof were hand made from choice timber. The puncheon floor of popular eventually gave way to narrow width maple. We even cemented the stones around the kitchen hearth, and one room got some fancy wallpaper, but newspapers and magazines sufficed for the other rooms.

We kept a few ducks and geese to furnish feathers for the "ticks" and pillows. The excitement of shearing sheep was an event. The most exciting event came when we "marked" the cattle and sheep before turning them loose to forage in the woods. This involved cutting notches (called varioudy and "under bit" "half crap" or "swallow fork" depending on size and shape) in the animal's ears. More enjoyable were tramps through the woods to salt the cattle. We never failed to keep a sharp look for red berries and distinctive leaves of ginseng or "sang" the roots of which were supposed by the Chinese to have valuable medicinal properties. (These roots could be sold for a big price).

Wood was plentiful and useful. Our meal barrels large enough for at least a bushel, was hand made, as was the mixing tray (bread bowl). Large trees split in half and hallowed out made excellent washtubs. Except for the barrel, our .22 caliber muzzle-loading rifle was completely hand made. The same was true of the shot pouch and bullet moulds, although we had to buy the percussion caps and powder. The banjo, down to its calfskin head, was strictly a local product. Out in the "lumber house", a general storage place, was a loom on which had been woven the numerous coverlids which were stacked away in the "big house" wooden shoe-lasts, used in an earlier day, littered the floor of the "lumber" house. Split hickory brooms and a little sandstone were sufficient for scrubbing floors, and split bottom chairs seemed to last indefinitely. To relieve the fatigue of adolescence, however, nothing surpassed the large sheepskin spread in the shade of the porch.

Up the creek a short distance, and not far from the sheep-house, was a water-powered mill for grinding corn. A millrace diverted the water to the wheel that turned the stones. If the water got low, we could use a public mill farther down the creek by paying a toll.

The noise and the vibration of the mill, the smell of the freshly ground meal as we ran it through our fingers to test for fineness are not easily forgotten.

There was a rugged independence in these people's minds and actions, the keynote however, was not individualism but cooperation was both a matter of practiced necessity and an avenue for social activity. Cooperation was for the general and individual good, not for the promotion of class interest. Class distinction in fact did not exist; every man was a capitalist, every man a laborer. Sympathy and a helping hand in time of distress were not matters for community agencies. It was spontaneous and natural gesture - the golden rule in practice. Midwife and other neighbors attended at childbirth. I never heard of a doctor being sent for on such occasions nor did I ever know of a mother dying at childbirth.

A death in the family meant the best curly maple or walnut wood - saved for such an event - was put in the hands of a good carpenter, who fashioned a simple coffin. The funeral was always held at the graveside and usually without a minister. People tended to live long. One of the first funerals I remember was "grandpap" Hannah, who died at the age of 90 after being confined to his bed for years, with a broken back. Uncle Tine died at the age of eighty-three, and Uncle Steve was over ninety. Times of rejoicing as well as sorrow brought the neighbors together. Weddings customarily came before birth; in any case the marriage tie was seldom broken except by death. A bride and groom were apt to be greeted by a charivari, which might include riding the groom on a rail - in his nightclothes - and dumping him in a cold creek. The first money I ever earned was by dancing at a Cataloochee wedding.

Perhaps this rural heaven did not offer the ideal life but it seemed good to those who lived it, and they wished for little else.

Homecoming on Cataloochee strikes a contrast between happy memories and the drab past. The Palmers and the Caldwells, the Messers and the Bennetts have departed. The acres they once tilled are covered by saplings (in 1950 now trees). The houses, now the abode of the bats and snakes, will soon be gone, identified only by the sentinel - like chimneys brooding - in stony silence over a lost land. Only when those with happy memories are gone will the present Cataloochee seem better than the old. (*Cataloochee Homecoming* by Robert H. Woody reprint in part. *The South Atlantic Quarterly* Vol. 49 No. 1 January 1950)

Dr. Woody became a History Professor and taught at Duke retired to California. Dr. Woody's now deceased but his words seem to paint a picture of the home life the way that it was and the way it remained for many years in Cataloochee. People were happy and thankful, never complaining of hard work, they were contented and counted their blessing for their accomplishments. It seems they were living better than most folks in those days.

Chapter 3

Ox Drawn Wagon to California

This story surely proves how much people loved to live in Cataloochee.

Daniel Cook was born on April 21, 1831 in eastern Tennessee, probably in the Cosby area. Sometime before 1854 he went to Big Cataloochee. He either went to work or for a visit Levi Colwell and his wife Mary Ann Naillon Colwell, they had three daughters at the time, and they were Harriett, Nancy Jane and Matilda.

Daniel soon began courting Harriett, who was born June 11, 1837. He may have traveled back and forth across Mt. Sterling or if he was working there he would have stayed with them. They were married July 24th 1854 but first Daniel had to take out a "marriage bond" for 500 pounds (English money) see copy of marriage bond. This amount is supposed to be "current money of the state." However the last account we have where English money (pounds, pence and etc) was 1822 in Waynesville, N.C.

<u>**APPENDIX B**</u>

MARRIAGE BOND AND LICENSE

FOR

DANIEL J. COOK AND HARRIET E. COLWELL

STATE OF NORTH CAROLINA.
Haywood County.

STATE OF NORTH CAROLINA,

KNOW ALL MEN BY THESE PRESENTS, That we Daniel J. Cook and James Williamson in the State aforesaid, are held and firmly bound to the State of North Carolina, in the just and full sum of FIVE HUNDRED POUNDS, current money of the State, to which payment well and truly to be made and done, we bind ourselves and each of us our heirs, executors and administrators jointly and severally, firmly by these presents sealed with our seals and dated the 24th day July A.D., 1854.

THE CONDITION OF THE OBLIGATION is such, That whereas the above bounden Daniel J. Cook hath made application for a License for Marriage, to be celebrated between him and Harriet E. Colwell of the aforesaid: nor in case it shall appear, hereafter, that there is any lawful cause to obstruct said marriage, the above obligation to be void; otherwise to remain in full force and virtue.

SIGNED, AND DELIVERED
IN PRESENCE OF

(signed) George Williamson
(signed) Danl. J. Cook/seal/

(signed) James Williamson/seal/

STATE OF NORTH CAROLINA,

Haywood County.

TO ANY REGULAR MINISTER OF THE GOSPEL, HAVING THE CARE OF SOULS, OF WHATEVER DENOMINATION - OR TO ANY JUSTICE OF THE PEACE OF SAID COUNTY:

You, or either of you, are hereby LICENSED AND AUTHORIZED to celebrate and solemnize the RITES OF MATRIMONEY between Daniel J. Cook and Harriet E. Colwell join them together as MAN AND WIFE.

WITNESS, William M Rhea Clerk of Haywood County Court, at

The 24th day of July A.D., 1854.

(signed) Wm M Rhea, Clk.

Marriage Bonds

In those days a man had to get permission from the girl's father to marry his daughter. He had to make a bond for a certain period of time, promising to be a good husband. If the promise was broken then he had to pay.

The English pound was used in this country, after the revolution some of the states started to mint their money. Massachusetts was the first to do so, then other states in the colonies started to do the same. There were some English pounds in use which became so confusing the U.S. Government started to mint all the money, but the pounds still had value, it took a long time to get all the pounds and state minted money converted into U.S. standard dollars.

Maybe Daniel had some pounds saved up or was it due to paper being so scarce that the old forms were used.

We have another copy of a marriage bond 1829 made by Evan Hannah for $1,000.00, which was twenty-five years earlier. This shows how difficult it was to deal with pounds and dollars.

Between 1820-1830 use of the pound was discontinued. 1822 is the last date we find where the pound was used in Waynesville, N.C.

Perhaps all the land in Big Cataloochee was taken, or maybe the land in Little Cataloochee was less expensive, at any rate Daniel and Harriett went over the Mountain and settled there on Coggin's Branch. They bought one hundred acres of land from the love Estate on the upper portion of Coggin's Branch

They built a beautiful log cabin. Daniel was known to be the best corner man around, that meant to have the ability to cut notches in the logs on each end to fit perfect with the next log, this is called dove tail.

In fact Daniel was a cabinetmaker and an expert in all kinds of woodwork. He built some of the furniture you will see pictures of in this book - he also made most of the shoes worn by his family

Harriett was an equally resourceful person. She wove cloth and made clothing, she grew and preserved food. She taught her daughters to weave beautiful coverlets with very fancy designs.

Granddaughter Joyce and Kenneth Reeves holding Daniel Cook's broadaxe

The floors were made of wide boards called puncheons, these were made of yellow poplar, which has a straight grain and could be split from the log with a froe. These boards were about four inches thick. The puncheons would be hand planed with a drawknife on one side to make a smooth floor.

When their house was finished, they needed a road to get back across the Mountain to Big Cataloochee and to haul in supplies, but there was only a trail.

Their neighbors in Little Cataloochee were Jack Vess who married Ruth Palmer, daughter of the first

George Palmer of Cataloochee. These two families in Little Cataloochee decided they would build a road. (Interview with Mark Hannah January, 1992)

While doing research I came across some of Mr. Wilbur's notes referring to the dug road, stating that it was 48 inches wide. Mark said, yes the road was dug out along the branch, some places did not require much digging, but some places they had to remove three or four feet of soil, rocks and roots. They used Maddox, shovels, hoes and a plow or anything to dig with. The road had to be 48 inches wide in order to get a narrow sled over it, to bring in supplies. The road ran from Davidson Gap down to the back of Palmer Chapel.

Harriett and Daniel had worked very hard but just could not get enough money to pay off the debt for the land. They had heard a man could get a good job paying good wages, working in timber industry in California.

This story is based upon a letter written by a granddaughter, Burdine Cook to Ola Messer Palmer, May 1, 1977.

Dear Cousain Ola,

Grandpa had built his house and was in debt. He said him and grandma had three children then they went to California in an ox drawn wagon to work in the redwood. It took them a year a going and a year a coming back. Grandma said they lived in a big stump cooked and eat and slept in that big stump two years, then paid their debt as soon as they returned to Little Cataloochee.

I worked two summers for your daddy (Will Messer) at the upper place at 25¢ a day. I was 10 or 12 years old and cood buy me a dress or a pair of shoes Saturday night with that $1.50. I thought I was rich.

Your Cousain

Burdine

Burdine Cook Childress,
Granddaughter of Daniel and Harriett Cook

Burdine Cook Childress lived to be almost 103 years old. When she was a small child her daddy died and Burdine went to live with her grandparents, the Cooks. The letter in part as interpreted by Ola's daughter Eunave Palmer Perkins. (Burdine's hand was very shaky due to age).

We know they would have spent time planning and preparing for such a long hard trip. They would need both summer and winter clothes because it would take a year to cross the desert and they would need enough food to last the whole trip.

As Daniel was an excellent wood worker, he was most likely busy making a big strong wagon for the near 3,000-mile trip. He probably would have gone back down to Cosby, Tennessee to build the wagon, because the Turnpike Road into Tennessee was not built until 1860. We have a letter from Joan Cook in Arkansas saying the story was passed to them that the Cooks were in California in 1857 and 1858.

If Daniel built the wagon in Tennessee, then somehow they would manage to get their supplies down there, probably on a narrow sled pulled by oxen. Harriett must have woven a canvas type cover for the wagon and making clothes for the family she would have used wool from the sheep's back (her father Levi had lots of sheep and probably gave her all the wool she needed).

After the wool was sheared from the sheep it had to be washed, dried, made into batts then spun into thread which would be woven into cloth, then the cloth would be dyed with indigo (blue) walnut hulls (brown) poke berries (rose) and various other plants were used for different colors. After all of this was done Harriett would cut out the pattern for their clothes and sew all of them by hand. That was just for their winter clothes.

Making their summer clothes was a big job too - first they had to grow flax then process it into thread, which was a long complicated procedure. After that she would weave it into cloth which would be pure linen or it could be woven with wool, then it was called woolsey-linsey or sometimes loosely woven with cotton for cooler clothes.

Harriett probably made plenty of lye soap to take along for doing laundry and bathing when water was available on their long trip across the desert.

Maybe Daniel found wild bees making honey in a hollow tree and gathered lots of honey to take along. They probably grew extra food, beans which could be strung on a string to dry in the hull called shuckey or leather britches. They would have taken as much corn meal and flour and cured pork as they had room for also dried apples, pumpkin, pepper and onions also potatoes.

They may have had a cow tied to the back of the wagon to furnish milk for the children, at least part of the way.

Daniel probably made beef or deer jerky to last most of the trip. Certainly he would have taken his gun and all the ammunition he had for their protection, and to add to their food supply at every chance. He probably took fish hooks and line; they would have fish when ever possible.

We wonder if other families went west with the Cooks, We know Jack Vess and his wife Ruth Palmer Vess and some of the Noland families, were all neighbors. Badger, Grady and Dave Noland all went out to Arlington, Washington according to their brother John Cordell Noland (interview 1992). He said Badger was the only one who returned. Maybe they all formed a wagon train and traveled together, especially through Indian Territory and the long hot trail across the desert, then over the steep mountain passes in freezing temperatures in winter. They probably traveled the Organ Trail to northern California. What tremendous courage and faith they had to start on such a journey. If these people traveled together they probably separated when they got out there and some went on to Arlington, Washington.

Jack Vess and his wife, Ruth Palmer Vess and Grady and Dave Noland and their families never returned, they continued to live there the rest of their life. We also found that Lear and Joe Price and some of the Halls of Cataloochee went out west.

This story is based upon the marriage record of Daniel J Cook and Harriett E Colwell July 25, 1854 and the letter from their granddaughter, Burdine Cook

Childress also a letter from a relative Joan Cook of DeQueen, Ark. The Cook children's birth dates according to the Haywood County census 1870, 1880, and 1900. Mary -born 1856, Sarah - 1858; Joseph- 1860, Regan - 1863, James- 1870, Harrison Riley - 1872, Hester- 1875, Rachel - 1876. Some children must have been born on the trip were not registered here when they returned. We are not sure of which years they traveled and which years they lived in California, anyhow the Cooks returned to Little Cataloochee and lived there the rest of their life.

Harriett died of pneumonia Oct. 25th 1903. Daniel died of cancer January 17th 1908. Both were buried in the cemetery of the Little Cataloochee Baptist Church.

As far as the Cooks preparing for their long journey, that is just a supposition. But nothing much changed in Cataloochee for one hundred years, and certainly that is kind of food they had and the way it was prepared and how they made their clothes.

After the Cooks returned from their long journey the nation was at war. Daniel served in Co. A 62nd N.C. Regiment. According to the roster, Daniel J. Cook was a Corporal. For more about this see *"Civil War Letters and Memories From the Great* Smoky *Mountains."* (By this same author) This regiment was formed in 1862. Daniel probably had to leave his pregnant wife, because their son Ragan was born in 1863 then it was seven years before another child was born James 1870, Harrison Riley 1872, Hester 1875 and Rachel 1876.

While Daniel was gone to war poor Harriett was left with all the children to care for to feed and keep warm, and another one on the way. She hunted and fished, chopped wood to cook with and warm the house, she made a garden, gathered wild berries and chestnuts.

Like other women during the War Harriett was left with all the responsibility and had to do men's work to survive.

Harriett's father Levi Colwell and her mother, Mary Ann (better known as Granny Pop) lived five miles away, across the Mountain, they most likely had been able to help her at first. Because her father was past 40 years of age and eleven children (we are not sure how many were still home) he was not conscripted to serve in the War.

Then two of Levis sons went to War, as the War lingered on, he helped as many women and children left alone as he could.

His oldest son left at home was Hiram 13 years old; he was strong and did lots of work too. Then they got word that Kirks marauders were coming across Mt. Sterling from Tennessee to take over Cataloochee.

Levi and Hiram rushed to help Mr. Howell and the home guard made up of old men and young boys. Levi was captured and taken away; Hiram young and strong was able to get away from the men on horses running after them. He slid down a very high creek bank then crawled under a thick patch of laurel and traveled a good distance before emerging to run home and tell the bad news.

Hiram would have to help his mother take care of all the other children. Poor Harriett left again with no help, but with lots of hard work she and all the children survived.

In 1865 Daniel returned and they bought an additional 31 acres and erected another house, which the family lived in for some 50 some years.

In 1891 Cook provided for the division of his property among three of his children. Rachel who married Will Messer 1894 received the home place and 43.38 acres and promised to care for her father and mother for as long as they lived.

Harrison R. received 52.86 acres and Hester received 35.25 acres. She married John Burgess in 1891 both established their own households on the remainder of the property, but in 1895 Harrison E. Cook sold his property to his sister Rachel and Will Messer and moved out of Little Cataloochee. Three of their daughters, Hester, Rachel and Sarah all had eleven children each.

More information has come to hand. Burdine Burgess Childress passed away December 24, 1986 she is buried in Deltona, Florida in Deltona Gardens. She had beautiful blue eyes; she lived to be 102 years old and missed 103 by only four months.

This information from Joan Cook, DeQueen, Ark.[1]

---

[1] All of this information pertaining to birth, death, marriage and land records from Dr. Roy Carroll, Raymond H. Pulley and others who researched and prepared the Historic Structures Report Little Cataloochee, North Carolina 1976 for the Great Smoky Mountain National Park

State of North Carolina,
YANCY COUNTY.

Court of Pleas & Quarter Sessions—January Term, 1857.

ORDERED by the Court, that the Heirs at Law of James Haney, deceased, be and they are hereby notified that the Sheriff has returned into this Court three hundred and sixty three acres of Land, lying and being in the county of Yancy, on the waters of Grassy Creek, adjoining lands of James Lowrey and others. Said land was returned into Court as the property of James Haney, deceased, to be sold for the tax due thereon, for the years 1852, '53, '54, and '55. Whole amount due, $15.50.

Issued 20th March, 1857.

Witness, DAVID McCANLES, Clerk.

March 26. Printer's fee $3.

Love Land

This advertisement of land for sale in 1857, the land was cheap, but money was very hard to come by. See the order by the court for the sheriff to sell 360 acres because the family could not pay $15.50 for the taxes on the property 1852-53-54-55. It was really hard to get money back then, they mostly lived by barter.

After the Civil was when many people lost their land and homes because they could not pay their tax, there was just not much money in the hands of the southerners.

300,000 ACRES
OF
LAND
FOR SALE!

By virtue of a Decree of the Court of Equity of Buncombe County, made in the case of James Gudger and others vs. James R. Love and others. I will expose to public sale at the following times and places THREE HUNDRED THOUSAND Acres of valuable Land, viz:

At Webster, Jackson county, on Tuesday of June Court, being the 16th day of the month, I will sell Fifty Thousand Acres, lying in Jackson county.

At Waynesville, Haywood county, on Tuesday the 23rd of June, I will sell One Hundred Thousand Acres, lying in Haywood county.

At Burnsville, Yancy county, on Monday the 20th day of July, I will offer for sale One Hundred Thousand Acres, lying in Yancy county.

At Jewel Hill, Madison county, on the 24th day of July, I will sell Fifty Thousand Acres, lying in Madison county.

The land will be divided into lots, and the sale will be continued at each place respectively from day to day until all is sold.

These lands are sold as the property of Robert Love, deceased, for the benefit of the heirs; and they embrace a great variety of soils and qualities, and are generally well suited to the growing of all the grains grasses, &c. Valuable mineral discoveries have been made on many parts of them, and there is reason to believe they contain inexhaustible stores of valuable metals. A minute description is deemed unnecessary, as those who wish to purchase will examine for themselves.

No better opportunity has ever been, nor probably ever will be, offered to the capitalist for the profitable investment of his money, or to the man of more limited means to secure a home in a healthy and desirable country.

Terms.

One, two and three years credit, with note and approved security. Title withheld until the purchase money is all paid.

L. B. SAWYER, C.M.E.

Appendix A

MARRIAGE BOND FOR EVAN HANNAH AND ELIZABETH NOLAND

STATE OF NORTH CAROLINA,

KNOW ALL MEN BY THESE PRESENTS, That we Evan Hannah and David Carver are jointly and severally held and firmly bound unto John Owen Esq. Governor, and his successors in office, for the time being, in the sum of ONE THOUSAND DOLLARS: to the payment of which well and truly to be made and done, we bind ourselves and each of us our heirs, executors and administrators jointly and severally, firmly by these presents sealed with our seals and dated the 31st day [sic] of April A.D. 1829.

The condition of the above obligation is such that whereas the above bounden Evan Hannah hath the day of the date hereof, applied for and obtained a license to marry with Elizabeth Noland Now if there be no lawful impediment to obstruct said marriage, then the above obligation to be void and of none effect, or otherwise to remain in full force and virtue.

attest

(signed) Rob. Deaver (his mark) Evan Hannah/seal/

(his mark) David Carver/seal/

Early Marriage bonds of Haywood County, 1808-1870, North Carolina Department of Archives and History, Raleigh, N.C.

Chapter 4

Uncle Steve Tells How it was 1866.

Steve Woody

Uncle Steve was interviewed in 1941, he was 90 years old, he recalled he was 10 years old, his father and other members of the family came to Cataloochee (Dr. Carroll's Research states that was 1866.

He said my daddy and mother had lived here before, but his mother became dissatisfied, she told daddy they couldn't raise children here, so they moved to Madison County near Hot Springs.

My mother had been dead bout five years when daddy decided to come back to the Valley. With four other small children we started out from Madison County in a wagon. It was a bad trip; there wasn't much of a road to follow in those days. We camped along the way and fixed our food whenever we stopped.

Few families in the Valley.

My daddy married the widow Caldwell (Mary Ann Naillon Colwell) who lived in the Valley after we came back here. There were only four or five families in here then. There was Fayte and Jessie Palmer, Young Bennett, Marion Caldwell and us.

I was raised in that little log house down in the Valley. There sure was a crowd of young ones in that house. The Widow Caldwell had eight, six of the boys were home and there were five of us.

Families in Cataloochee in those days raised practically everything they used, but once in a while they had to go outside to get a few things they couldn't produce.

We raised all the food we needed, but we went out of the Valley to Canton every two months or so. We had to use a two-horse team to get over the mountains and it was an all day trip. We did our trading at night, got a few little things we needed and took the rest for our stuff in money. Then we would start back early next morning and it was another all day trip back.

No Trouble Making a Living

There wasn't any trouble making a living in the Valley. I never heard of a fellow over here borrowing money. But people from other places would come in here to borrow it. Most people in the Valley in those days kept their money at home, they didn't seem to like the idea of having it in a bank somewhere way off.

This was a right substantial Valley. Did you know before the Park took over the land, that Cataloochee Township paid the second highest tax in Haywood

County? Waynesville was the first. I was the tax collector in this township for 18 years.

Cataloochee in those days was a sportsman's paradise. Game was here in droves. Deer used to roam about the Valley in regular herds and it wasn't any trouble at all to kill one when you needed meat. But just all at once the deer just up and left. That was about 35 years ago. Nobody knows why.

Wolves and bears used to pester the sheep a lot. They wouldn't bother the cows, but we had to put the sheep up every night. We left the sheep out one night and the wolves came after the sheep, we took out after them and up in the long yellow patch we killed six of them.

There were plenty of wildcats in here then too, and there was a lot of possum and mink, we did a lot of trapping in those days.

There also were a lot of bears in here then, but are more now (after the Park took over). Bears, they are just laying around in these orchards people moved off and left. We never were without bear meat when we wanted it.

This country hasn't ever been cut over. Uncle continued pointing to the virgin timber that comes down close to his home. When we come here very little of the fields were cleared. You just moved in and cleared a place for your cabin and a little garden and then you kept working until you cleared more and more land.

We had a good school in here too. It had two rooms and we had two teachers and about 60 pupils. We have only one teacher here now and just 11 children at school. It won't be long before there won't be any. The government lets us live on our land, they lease it to us each year and when we die it won't be leased anymore.

Always Glad to Get Home

Uncle Steve leaves the Valley a couple of times a year to spend a few days with his son in Waynesville but always glad to get back home. He is deep rooted into Cataloochee Valley, and plans to live out his years in the section he knows so well. No other place could seem like home.

On a recent (1941) visit to Cataloochee Valley, Newton B. Drury, director of the National Park Service, remarked that the Park areas are set aside only because they have an element of greatness and Cataloochee he said is one of those great places which must be preserved as much as possible in its natural state, a Valley where man sorely beset by troubles of an imperfect world may retreat and gain a new prospective, a greater vision a Shangri-La where the best must be preserved in order that this and future generations may go there and find a new faith in greatness of America. (Source: *The Asheville Citizen* 1941)

Levi's Headstone

Levi and Mary Ann Naillon Colwell are buried side by side in the cemetery high on the hill behind the church.

Evidently there had been some controversy about who were the first permanent residents of Cataloochee. According to Dr. Roy Carroll's research Levi Colwell and Young Bennett and Jimmy Colwell were the first permanent settlers and here is an inscription on Levi's headstone. On the backside of it reads:

Members of the M.E. Church South One of the first three Families settled on Cataloochee about 1836

Mary Ann is buried beside Levi.

In Dr. Carroll's research he found there was a place in Cataloochee called the Hannah Fields, he found no record of them living there permanently until 1839 when Evan Hannah and family came there with William Reddy Noland's family. They first lived on the south side of Cataloochee Creek below the iron bridge.

Most surely they had been coming there several years before, at least in the summer and fall to have cleared a field and for it to be known as the Hannah Fields. I have made many inquires and found that the fields referred to was a large flat area along Boogerman Trail.

These two families could have lived there first while they were ranging cattle on the grassy balds and growing gardens in the rich virgin soil.

Dr. Carroll also found that some place was referred to as Barnes Camp. We have not been able to locate that area.

Cataloochee Valley Family Reunion

August 13, 1989
Speech by: Myron L. Coulter
Chancellor Western Carolina University

How fortunate you all are to be members of the Woody, Messer, Palmer, Caldwell, Cook, Hannah and other families who settled and flourished in these beautiful surroundings. How fortunate are we, who are not members of your families, that you take the time and make the effort to honor your ancestors, their homesteads, their resting places, and their legacies for all of us.

Indeed, the setting of this valley is distinctive and beautiful. Isn't it wonderful that through out our land we are so privileged to have a myriad such places where our forefathers pioneered and established their homes, and became productive developers of this great nation?

But you, here in Cataloochee, are even more distinctive. You choose not to let go of your heritage. Where others have let nature reclaim and obliterate all traces of our original settlements, you have elected to cooperate with that same nature in preserving both the heritage of your family - founders of the lovely place, which was home to them. In that respect, and many others, you are unique. You care; you want to perpetuate the tangible reminders of life and family, which those pioneer women and men gave to you. You come here at least annually to remind yourselves and all others that there were once families here, your families, who came to this valley where no homes or farms existed -- where there were no pre-established means of making a living or raising a family. You are continually honoring the initiative, the fortitude, the tenacity, to commitment to wrench the means of survival from a sometimes hostile, always challenging expanse of forest and mountain.

As I entered the Cataloochee Valley for the first time, I was immediately taken back in my mind to the earlier, less cluttered times in our culture. I thought of a time when there was no bus, no car, and no airplane to take us from place to place.

I thought of a time when there was no harnessed electric power, no telephones, no radio, no television to light our homes or carry our voices and images beyond the range of our eyes and ears.

If there was ever a time when the family needs to reestablish itself as the center of our culture, it is now.

Thank goodness the families of Cataloochee have not let the traditions, the history, the importance of the family drift out of existence. Thank goodness we have people such as John Parris who are establishing an oral and a recorded chronicle of life in these mountains. And thank goodness each year you observe the importance of the individual, the patriarchs, the matriarchs, the settlers of this valley and their descendants. You have kept the tradition alive while others are now trying to revive their traditions. You are preserving your heritage. You have maintained and honored the spirit of the Cataloochee families.

Today in this place you are communicating. You are showing your children and your guest by example. You are using different ways to express your values, both material and spiritual. You are revisiting and renewing your roots. You are imprinting your past and cultural values upon others as they were imprinted upon you by those hundreds of hardy men and women who made this valley come alive and become an essential partner in their lives.

There have been many speeches. Included here are just a few of the speeches that have been made at the reunion, there have been many very impressive speakers and we want to express our thanks for them coming and for their expressions of appreciation of our heritage.

Chapter 5

Education and Schools in Cataloochee Township

Address by Dr. Roy Carroll UNC Chapel Hill
At the Cataloochee Reunion, August 11, 1991.

Dr. Carroll gave all the statistics on these schools and spoke of their closing.

He said, the focus for the communities were gone. But those rural schools were far more than cultural centers for their communities. James Rooney captured their significance well in his book with that marvelous title. *Journey From Ignorant Ridge* (1976). He wrote of the little country schoolhouse, which he attended:

It seemed, as I recall it, a lonely little house of scholarship, with its playground worn so bare, that even the months of sun and idleness failed to bring forth any grass. But that humble little school had a dignity of a fixed and far-off purpose... It was the outpost of civilization. It was the advance guard of the pioneer, driving the wilderness further west. It was life preparing wistfully for the future.

Dr. Carroll said, "That's it exactly." The people of Cataloochee invested their labor and love in their schools and churches. The Beech Grove School, Palmers Chapel, and the Little Cataloochee Baptist Church were the work of their hands, and they remain as mute but powerful symbols of their faith and their hope for the future.

The 90th Psalm, an eloquent testimony to the transience of life, ends with a prayer of another people long ago: "Yea, Lord, the work of our hands, establish thou it."

Dr. Carroll finished his speech with this: The tolling of the church bell this morning, as at every annual gathering, reminds us that people born in this valley are disappearing year by year. These reunions were started and sustained by them as a homecoming, as a reminder of who they were, where they came from, and what they wrought in these beautiful mountains.

I urge you to keep this tradition and that memory alive, and thus in some small measure, to establish the work of their hands. (For complete speech see p. 123 of "*Reflections of Cataloochee*" it was shortened due to space.)

Schooling

This is a letter from a Cataloochee descendant, Carolyn Bennett Mahaffey of Atlanta, Ga., she is employed at Georgia Tech, she wrote:

Dear Hattie:

I was delighted to hear that you are writing a book on Cataloochee. It's good to preserve all that can be found, since it is a lost time and place otherwise. From what I can learn, it was something really unique, and represents many of the qualities that our country has lost today - the working together to build a community, the foundation in a religious faith, the honest dealings people seemed to have with one another, and the work ethic. One of my distant cousins sent me a picture of a class of children in the one-room school at Cataloochee, most of them barefoot and certainly "backwoods" by any standard. Yet, many of those children went on to become anything from prosperous farmers to doctors and dentists to schoolteachers and who knows what else. Now we hear people here today blaming all the ills of society on the lack of funds for the school and a thousand other failures of society to provide what is needed to educate today's kids. What do you suppose makes the difference??? There is much we could learn from those 100 years from Cataloochee's first settlers to its end after the Park Service took it over.

This Writer's Answer:

I believe the difference was the old-fashioned virtues and morals based upon honesty, discipline and respect, all according to their religious beliefs. The children were disciplined in various forms. They got little spankings for misbehaving. They got a whipping with a switch if they did a mean thing, but they were not beaten. I never heard of anyone being cruel to their children. It hurt the parents worse than the child, but they knew if the child was not disciplined that he would have a troubled life.

Whipping and paddling were not always used - sometimes they had to stand in the corner, or could not go play with the other children or they got dishwashing duty.

This writer never heard any cussing or foul language until many years after we moved from Cataloochee.

In those plain little one or two room schools, the teachers were caring, they taught well. The children knew they were expected to learn and not cause the teacher any trouble. The teacher was allowed to paddle any who caused trouble or disobeyed or if the pupils did not do their homework, the parents approved of her paddling their child if he needed it.

Floyd Woody was a mischievous fellow, always having fun - he chuckled and said, yeah, I got some whippings at school and sometimes, another one when I got home because I got one at school (Interview 1989). The parents felt like it would be a reflection on them if they didn't teach their children good manners and good behavior. I believe the home schooling and the public schooling were both important, the parents set good examples.

We never heard people grumbling or self-pitying about having to work. Everyone accepted whatever job they needed to get done. They tackled it with great enthusiasm and pride. Their homes and farms looked much like an Amish Village, all neat and clean. They loved the good land and the good things they could grow. They helped each other, laughing and joking as they worked. The big jobs seemed small, with everyone working together.

This work ethic was instilled in them when they were small children. When the adult went to carry in a big load of wood, the child went along, he or she would be given a few sticks of kindling wood to carry. The child would be told that he or she was such a big help. If the adult went to carry in a bucket of water, the child would be given a small bucket to help. If the adult went to the springhouse to get a bucket of milk, the child got to carry the butter or something small.

The children were included with most of the work, and they were made to feel important for helping. As they grew older the jobs became bigger but they did not mind.

This work taught the children responsibility and they knew they could accomplish anything they wanted to. All of this training must come in the early years of their life, before other things crowd their mind.

Of course that was long before television was every thought of.

At any rate many who were born in Cataloochee went out into the world, went to schools and colleges and became very successful businessmen or professionals in many fields and successful farmers.

Yes the children were disciplined but they were also shown love and kindness.

The children often sat on someone's lap, Mothers, Daddy's, Aunts, Uncles or who ever was around. When the babies were sleepy they would be rocked to sleep, usually by their mother, who sang a lullaby. "Rock-a-by-baby in a tree top, when the wind blows the cradle will rock, when the bow breaks down comes baby cradle and all." (Brahms Lullaby? Same tune)

In wintertime they all sat around the fireplace talking, children in their laps. Before they were put to bed at night, the children's feet would be warmed real good then carried to bed and be tucked in. The children said their prayers and said goodnight, then the kerosene lamp was blown out (the flame).

There was no electric blankets or even any insulation in the walls, only the fireplaces for heat. Most everyone had feather beds; ticks filled with down (tiny feathers) these were cozy for sleeping. When the weather was real cold the flat irons (used for ironing clothes) would be heated by placing them close to the fire in fireplace. When the iron was hot a thick cloth would be wrapped around it, then it would be placed in the bed, near their feet. Some people who didn't have ducks or geese to pick the down to make the feather beds would use straw or finely shredded shucks. Many had quilts padded with wool, and wool blankets.

Yes home schooling and the plain little one or two room schools laid a firm foundation for their children and they knew they could accomplish anything they wanted to. I give credit to the loving, caring parents and dedicated teachers.

Little Cataloochee School 1908?
Ola, North Carolina
Miss Cora Hawkins, (teacher)

Student's names in preceding picture

Front Row L to R

1 Willie M. Messer

2 Jarvis Bennett

3 Troy Burgess

4 Owen Burgess

5 Manson Conrad

7 Thurman Conard

8 Fred L. Hannah

Second Row L to R

9 Ollie Belle Messer

10 Eva Messer - Mrs. T.L. Sharp

11 Addie Lockmon - Mrs. Sidney Nelson Sr

12 Nicey Conard

13 RoyH.Hannah

14 Robert V. Hannah

15 Herman Burgess

Third Row L to R

22 Mont M. Hannah

23 Allen Hall

24 Charles Bennett

25 Weaver Bennett

26 James Bennett

27 Robert M. Hannah

28 Floyd Burgess

29 Glenn Bennett

30 Jas. Tine Bennett

Fourth Row L to R

31 J. Thurman Hannah

32 Laura Hannah - Mrs. Dunn

33 Ora Hanna Mrs. Levi Calwell

34 Elizabeth Bennett - Mrs. Bremmer

35 Iva Lee Hannah - Mrs. W.B. Bennett

36 Cora Hawkins (Teacher) Mrs. Robert Bennett

16 Gola Bennett

17 Dock Milas Bennett

18 Loretta Messer - Mrs. C. L. Valentine

19 Unidentified

20 Lela Bennett - Mrs. Clark

21 Ella Mae Hall - Mrs. Floyd Plemmons

37 Nettie Smith - Mrs. C. Caldwell

38 Dora Burgess

39 Flora Messer - Mrs. C.L. Norrow

40 Joe Estuce Hannah

41 Homer Lockmon

Photo Courtesy of Mildred Hannah Hazel Fairfax. VA.

Memories of Little Cataloochee
By Beatrice Burgess Palmer Sisk

Beatrice Burgess Palmer Sisk - granddaughter of Daniel Cook - born Feb. 14, 1911

"Childhood Memories" October 1998
"And That's The Way It Was in Little Cataloochee Valley When I grew Up"
By Beatrice Sisk

I had a wonderful childhood when I grew up, a good mother and dad, little brothers, and three of us girls. So you can imagine how much work went on in a family of 13.

My mother was a sister to Aunt Rachel Cook Messer, she and Uncle Will also had 11 children. It was always a joy to spend a night in their home, after the chores were done Aunt Rachel would gather us kids around the fireplace in the wintertime and tell us tall tales and ghost stories. I would be so scared when I went to bed I would pull the covers over my head and keep my eyes closed so I wouldn't see the ghosts she told us about.

In our house we obeyed our parents. We were taught to tell the truth, not to use bad language, not to steal. Not to take God's name in vain, if Mom and Dad had company come in we had to get up give the visitors our chairs, go out and play. Also we were not allowed to call the older people by their given name, it had to be Mr. And Mrs. or Aunt and Uncle.

We never had a lot of things like people have today, but we had love and understanding, we all worked together and helped each other. I hear kids today asking their mothers, what can I wear to school today. What can I wear to church on Sunday, I have nothing to wear. Just take a peep inside their closets, most of the time it's filled to overflowing, but Mom it's not new. When I hear words like this I want to tell them that I never had to ask Mom what dress I could wear to church on Sunday, I only had two Sunday dresses. I wore one, one Sunday; the next Sunday I wore the other one.

My mother always told us children "That fine feathers don't make fine birds."

Where we went school was a good-sized building with a stage all the way across the back of the building, this is where we had our classes. Benches were across one end of the stage, with blackboards fastened on the wall, where we worked arithmetic problems and did other school work. Where spelling classes were called on stage, we stood in a line, the teacher gave out the words, if someone missed a word, it was then passed on to the next person, if they spelled the word, that person got to move above the one that missed the word, when you finally made it to the head of the class you were given a head mark by the teacher in a little book she, or he, kept themselves at the end of the school year, the person that had the most head marks, were given a little gift by the teacher. One year I happened to be the lucky one and was given a little book by my teacher, Fred Hannah, I was so proud of that and had it for many years. He was the best teacher, and taught me more than any other teacher I had. We always begin each school day by singing a song and repeating "The Lord's Prayer."

In our school we had no running water, no inside bathrooms, no electric lights. We had a long cast iron wood stove, didn't heat the building very well, if the weather was very cold the teacher would allow us to move up closer to the stove so we would be more comfortable. We had large desks that seated two people, which had an ink well built in, with a cover over the top of the ink, where you dipped an old fashioned ink pen every minute or so, most of the time we just used a pencil. I remember making ink out of pokeberries which grew wild in the fields during autumn, it sure wasn't blue - but bright red. To be excused to go to the outhouse we had to get permission by holding up our hand and asking "may I be excused?"

We had a recess of about 30 minutes both morning and afternoon, on each Friday about three o'clock we put away our books and had to participate in a little talent show. We would have a spelling contest to see who could stand up and spell the longest, sing songs, say speeches, or what ever. If you refused to take part in some activity, come Monday morning, you would have to stay in and study while the rest were out playing. On one occasion I needed something to do or say for Friday talent show so my Dad taught me a little speech, and I quote:

"Monkey setting on the end of a rail picking his teeth with the end of his tail. Mulberry leaves and calico sleeves all the school teachers are so hard to please."

As I think back on that now, she could have punished me, but she was kind and didn't. On the school playground we had a huge chestnut tree, beneath the tree was a large flat surface where we played many games, such as tap hand, ring around the roses, drop the handkerchief, farmer in the dell, what's your occupation, and many more. This was also where we jumped the rope only we had no ropes like kids have today. Let me tell you what we did have. They were called ginger ropes, it grew in the woods, came up out of the ground, ran up the big trees and across the tree branches, you could cut them off at the ground and pull them out of the trees, you could find them in small, medium or large sizes, we liked the small or medium size, they were not so hard to turn. These ginger ropes would grow long enough so 4 or 5 people could be jumping the rope at the same time if they so desired.

We had a lot of fun, all (home made) no cost involved, just imagination and some hard work. We also played baseball. We also made our own bats and balls. In making our balls we would just find a small round rock for the center then we would take yarn and begin rolling it around and all over, being careful to keep it the same size all over until it was as large as we wanted, next we would take a large needle with strong thread and began sewing through and over and all around, over and over, until we were sure it would not come apart. We spent many happy hours playing with things we made ourselves. At this time in life we had no way of going to town, no cars, some few people did ride horses into town on business, but not very often.

We were a happy, healthy group of kids. No smoking. No drinking, No dope. No drugs and all those other things that children have to deal with today. We always had to walk to school. No snow days off, if it snowed knee deep we still went to school, no buses, as time went on we did have better roads, trucks, and cars, which was a blessing, but we still had the deep snows. We would make our picture in the snow by stretching out our arms away from our body and falling backward in the big snowdrift, which left an imprint of our body, (or our picture as we called it) in the snow. "Wonderful memories"

We made our sleds we rode down the hill on; some small, some large enough two or three could ride on them. It was fun making our own playthings. I only had one store bought doll, my brother Floyd after he grew up and got a job, bought my sister, Cora and I a beautiful doll for Christmas. One had blond hair and blue eyes that would open and close, its dress was pink with little white slippers and the other one had black hair and eyes. Its dress was blue with black slippers. We loved them so much, we wouldn't play with them, they were about 12 inches tall and came fastened in boxes. We set them up above the fireplace on the mantle where we could look at them all the time. We thought they were the prettiest dolls in the world. We made rag dolls we played with all the time, painted their eyes, nose and mouth with ink also made their dresses, and used black ink for dark curly hair. Not real pretty to look at sometimes, but we were proud of them because we made them.

We also made our playhouses under a fig tree near the woods, in a barn or in an empty building. For our rugs on the floor we would go into the woods and pull off the green moss off of the logs that had fallen down years before, cover the ground, made a nice soft rug. We also made little beds out of moss. We would roll it up the size we wanted, place it where we wanted then take a larger piece, spread it over the top for a bedspread, then roll up more moss laid it across the top for pillows and they were cute. We had no tea sets for dishes, so we would search around homes, for broken dishes, tin can or what ever we could find to make it look more home life. We drew pictures, and drove up a peg, and hung them up. We spent many happy hours planning and playing in our playhouses.

We also made some music along the way, our school teacher taught us to take a comb you use for your hair, put tissue over it, put it to your lips and hum a song. At the close of school one year all of us learned the song of "The Wreck of the Great Titanic". This was when the parents came for our little program. We were all on the stage together and did this song. Some sang the words; others used the combs to make the music. Can't remember how old I was at that time, but I do remember how proud I was of our little country school.

Another thing we didn't have in our homes was running water. We did have a spring, bubbling up out of the ground nearby the homes, which had to be dug out deep, then a cover built over to keep out rain water, leaves or whatever, then a spring house was built as close to the spring as possible, the overflow of spring water ran into the springhouse into a long box the length of the house and overflowed at the bottom. This was where we kept our milk, butter, eggs or anything we wanted to keep cold. We used buckets and stone crocks all were covered with lids, placed them down in the cold water, and really kept everything nice and cold. Mother always said where there is a will, there is a way, this has also proven true in my life also. So many good things have come my way, along with the sad times too, but the good out weighs the bad.

I am so thankful that I have lived in a time that I think has been the greatest in the history of the world. So many great things have been accomplished during my lifetime, with many more great things to be done if keep on "keeping on" there is always, "The Reward of Perseverance"

Two frogs fell into a deep cream bowl,
One was wise and a cherry soul,
The other one took a gloomy view,
And bade his friends a sad adieu.
Said the other frog with a merry grin
" I can't get out but I won't give in;
I'll swim around till my strength is spent,
Then I'll die the more content."
And as he swam, though ever it seemed,
His struggling began to churn the cream.
Until on top of pure butter he stopped.
And out of the bowl he quickly hopped.

The moral you ask? Oh it's easy found, if you can't get out, keep swimming around. Let's never give up, when we are discouraged but keep on until the victory is won. The promise is to the "FAITHFUL" when the going gets tough "KEEP ON SWIMMING".

Bee Burgess Palmer Sisk

Taped Speech at 1977 Cataloochee Homecoming

Speaker: Honorable Lamar Gudger, Congressman, US House of Representatives, N.C. 11th Congressional District (Western North Carolina)

This annual Cataloochee homecoming tradition here in Cataloochee Valley symbolizes what is right with America. Why do I mention this? Because this coming back home, this meeting together, assures that we retain the traditional respect for family, the traditional respect for brotherhood, traditional respect for our faith that makes us strong, that makes us great.

The tolling of the bell, of which we have just heard, was a stirring experience for me. It was a beautiful memorial in honor of the twelve members of this brotherhood and community who have passed away since last year.

In the passing of each old friend, there is a sense of anguish but this is God's way of bringing back home to Him those who are a part of His brotherhood just as this homecoming tradition brings back home those of you with your roots affixed to Cataloochee Valley.

I rejoice that this church stands here in good repair. I rejoice that you have a place you can reconvene with families that once made up this Christian community, and still adhere to this sense of brotherhood and a sense of significance. I grew up my summers on the farm, just as many of you did, and no one can live on the farm, and no one can live in a community like this without knowing God is here, without knowing that there are things that we cannot explain. We explain it through Him, knowing that He has blessed our nation beyond any others.

I hope that someday this church may become a historical monument. I would like to see more of these same ideas perpetuated here. And don't forget that the National Park Service is committed to not merely protecting primitive wild land conditions, but also historic matters. And I would like to think what we are doing here today, will be done fifty years from today by your descendants and a hundred years from today by their descendents.

If we can just keep coming home, America: If we can just keep worshiping God. America: and if we can just keep our faith in our God and in ourselves, America: We're going to be all right. But we must be on God's side. We must adhere to our faith. We must seek first His righteousness and all else shall then be added unto us.

I thank you for letting me be here with you. I thank you for trusting me to represent you in Congress and I thank you for letting me share my thoughts with you today.

This is a beautiful symbol represented here today. One that allows us to enter the third century in our nation's history with songs on our lips and a ringing bell - both echoing up and down the green valleys and mountains of Cataloochee and the Great Smokies.

Again thank you for the opportunity to meet with you today in this beautiful place, for this annual tradition we hope will go on and on in America's future.[1]

---

[1] Location: Palmer Chapel, Cataloochee, N.C. Great Smoky Mountain National Park. Date: August 1977 (11 a.m.). Taped by John Palmer, Seasonal Park Naturalist (summer '76 & '77) assigned to Cosby and Cataloochee Districts.

Chapter 6

The People of Cataloochee

George Palmer (Turkey George)

Turkey George Palmer in his young days. Much has been written about him. He was a famous bear hunter; legend is that he killed 105 bears.

He got his nickname of turkey due to his building a pen to capture wild turkeys (see *Reflections of Cataloochee).*

Turkey George would never give up Cataloochee, no matter what restrictions the Park put on him, he lived there until he died and was buried there. He married Uncle Andy Caldwell's daughter, Alice. They lived up Indian Creek (now Palmer Creek) near Pretty Holler Creek.

Will Never Give Up Cataloochee

Vaughn Palmer 100 years old (2002)

These photos were made at Palmer Chapel August 2002 at the Cataloochee Reunion. When the people had to leave their beloved homeland, they made a pact between them that they would never give up Cataloochee. You can see here that they meant what they said. There were others on walkers and some with canes. They were from 100 years old down to a two months old baby boy. Jonathan Palmer West, the first grand child of Steven Woody. There could have been some younger, the crowd was so large we couldn't tell.

Thad Sutton
86 years old (2001)

Larry Caldwell - age 79 (2001)

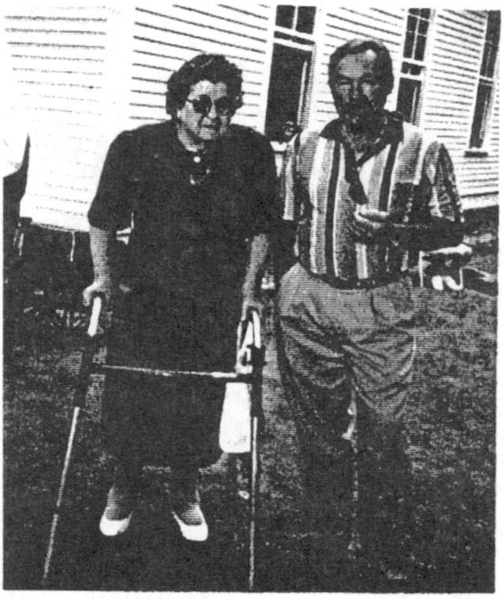

Mrs. Earl Messer and son Ralph
2001

Mary Lou Leatherwood
2001

Front Row: L to R: Magola Caldwell with baby, unidentified, Frank Rogers teacher, with baby.

Back Row: L to R: Willie Medford Rogers and baby, unidentified, Charlie Ray Caldwell, Ruth Smathers, teacher, Vaughn Palmer. Photo courtesy of Douglas Smathers, Canton.

Creek George & Martha Russell Palmer, baby Lawrence, Middle Elmer Girl, on left Myrtle (Camp), girl on right Della (Compton) Back row: Ethel (McCracken), Jarivs, Lura & David

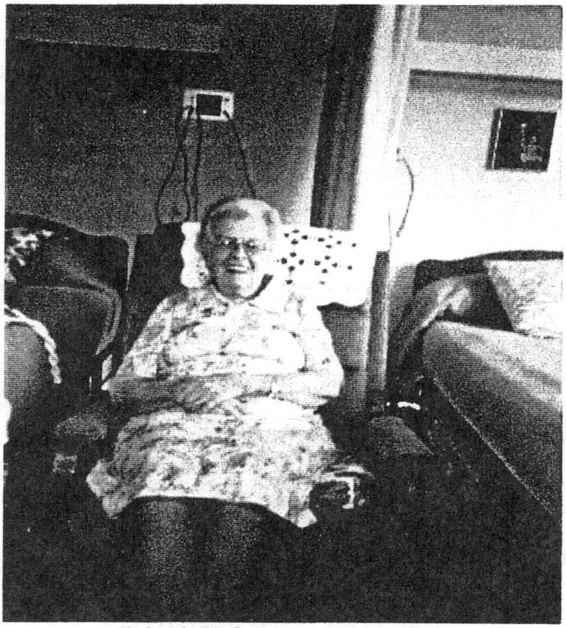

Ethel Palmer McCracken

Buggies

I talked with Mrs. Ethel Palmer McCracken, born on Big Cataloochee 1894, about buggies. "Oh yes several people had them, when we left, moving out of Cataloochee in 1920. I drove the buggy and took mother out." Ethel was 26 years old then. I asked her how long it took her to drive the buggy from Big Cataloochee to Ratcliff Cove near Waynesville; she said, "Well it took most of a day. It was a right hard trip on Mother."

I asked how many people had buggies? "Why it seems like just about every family had one, Aunt Mag Caldwell, Jarvis Palmer, Aunt Lizzie Caldwell, Aunt Mila

Palmer, Steve Woody, lots of folks had them, and back then 1920 and before, we didn't hardly ever see a car in Cataloochee. Our traffic was horse and buggy, wagons and horses, people riding horses. Of course they walked anywhere they wanted to go, if the horse was in use."

In 1920 George Palmer and his family moved to Ratcliff Cove, near Waynesville, N.C. We talked about moving furniture and farm equipment. She said, "Well our bedding was mostly feather beds and some straw ticks (Mattresses). They loaded them and other things in covered wagons. I guess everything else was hauled out in regular wagons. You know we had so many things to farm with. Mowing machine, hay rake, turning plow and hammers and hoes and just all kinds of things, single foot plows, corn sheller and I don't remember what all. Well yes, we had a big Home Comfort Cook stove and a Warm Morning heater, I don't know how many trips daddy (Creek George) and the boys had to make across that mountain to haul everything out."

Of course they drove all the livestock out on foot over the mountain all the way to Ratcliff Cove. Her father George was superintendent of Sunday school several years. He always took all of them to church; sometimes they would walk, sometimes he would take them in the wagon. He also served on the school committee he was concerned with the welfare of the community.

Mrs. McCracken spoke of riding sidesaddle and wearing long skirts. Later I played hymns in church. Us children raised pigs, when we sold them we bought an organ, Myrtle Medford, our cousin taught us to play by shaped notes, none of them round things, sharps and flats. A Mr. Killian came over there and taught singing.

We talked about Thanksgiving. Why we didn't have anything special, we always gave thanks, and we always had plenty to eat and we could set a table for anybody, anytime. Now days you would have to run to the store to fix a good dinner.

She spoke of picnicking, singing, good food, horseback riding and how kind everyone was in Cataloochee. "Why people don't know anything about living now days, good living that is." She said.

Palmer Family

Sunday afternoon at Creek George Palmers.

L to R: Creek George, Dau. Laura Jarrett, Will Maria, Harley, John, Polly, Jim and Jarvis

Photo: Courtesy of Mrs. Ethel Palmer McCracken

We always had singing school in summer. A Mr. Long from Cove Creek would come to Cataloochee and teach the singing. He had what they called a tuning fork; he would slide a little bar down to C or what ever key he wanted, then he would strike the thing, hold it to his ear, this gave him the correct key to start the song.

We always looked forward to our singing, it was a lot of fun, a social function you know. Sometimes daddy would take a wagonload of us to church to practice our singing, or to Sunday school.

We asked her if she ever drove a car, she said "no, but I was foolish enough to try once." She smiled as she recalled, "I run it into the bank, I tell you I quit right then and there, never tried it again!" What kind of a car was it we asked, she said "Well some fellow there in the Radcliff Cove was lucky enough to get some kind of a little car back then, a Model A or Model T Ford. I don't know which. We were sort of courting, he wanted to teach me to drive, well when I hit that bank that was enough for me! It scared me." (Remember this is the lady that thought nothing of driving a horse and buggy with her mother, up that winding steep road over Cove Creek Mountain more than 4,500 ft. elevation and down the other side into Waynesville and beyond to Radcliff Cove.)

Making Dentures

Mrs. Ethel Palmer McCracken moved out of Big Cataloochee, along with her family in 1920. She and her sister, Myrtle went to work at Waynesville's first hospital, which was a large house on Pigeon Street. They trained to be nurses. After working there a while she married Cramer McCracken and they moved to Big Branch, near Clyde. One day a neighbor came to their house with a magazine called "Home Comfort." "This must have been 1924 or 1925" Mrs. McCracken said, "this poor lady did not have any teeth and she showed me that magazine, there was an ad to order material, to make false teeth. Well, I had never done anything like that and told her I didn't know anything about making teeth, but she told me that she knew I could do anything and she needed the teeth so bad and could not afford to go to a dentist. Well, I agreed. So we wrote off for the material and in just a few days we received enough material to make the upper impression. I read the instructions; we put a little girl in the floor with a clock to time my work. I got the stuff mixed up and put it in her mouth. The poor lady had palsy or something that made her head shake. I had to hold her head with one arm and hold the tray of stuff in her mouth with the other hand. Then it was pretty soon time to take it out, well that thing was stuck in her mouth, but I finally wiggled it out. We sent it off and it was accepted, then we wrote for material to make an impression for the lower plate. We soon got it back and I followed the same procedure, we sent it off, but they wrote that it was imperfect. First they had sent a wad of stuff to get the bite. The second time we made the lower impression it was ok. They sent it back and it fit good with the upper. The cost was $18.00 and they never hurt her mouth and she never did have an adjustment, and they looked as good as my $100 set of dentures. Then I got worried, they might get me for practicing without a licenses."

Mrs. McCracken was 102 years of age February 1996. She has a remarkable memory and she still sews, she had a made a round cushion by hand. She is not crippled but she is walking now on her mother's walker, just to be on the safe side. She is looking forward to attending the Cataloochee reunion in August. (Interview with Mrs. McCracken 4-19-96)

Note: Mrs. McCracken is always cheerful, it is a pleasure to visit her. She was the calendar girl 1995; they had a nice color picture of her on the calendar at Brian Center.

Toothbrushes

Mrs. Ethel Palmer (McCracken) spoke of their first toothbrushes. She said you know how good the sweet birch tasted; we would break off nice tender sticks and chew one end until it was nice and soft. Then we would dip it in a little baking soda and scrub our teeth, then rinse our mouth. It really did clean our teeth and we did this real often, I guess I was about 12 years old when we went to visit some of our neighbors, they had the same kind of tooth brush as we did and everyone of them had the prettiest white teeth you ever saw. I discovered they were dipping Bruton Snuff, well I thinks to myself, I believe I will try that, make my teeth as white as theirs. I had my birch tooth brush chewed just right. I dipped it in someone's box of snuff and turned it around till it looked like a mop. Now I stuck that in my mouth and started brushing, soon I got dizzy and sick, just awfully sick, I wished I could vomit, but I couldn't. I was just staggering all around and fell in a big bin of wool, where they had just sheared the sheep. My sister found me; she helped me out and got some water to wash my mouth out with. I'll tell you that cured me, I never had any desire to dip snuff after that and still can't stand the scent of it.

Now people have heard awful things about us mountain people. You tell them (in your book) that we were strong, straight, well built people and we were not cross-eyed or bow legged and that we all had nice straight teeth. Tell them to look at our pictures, and then they can see for themselves.

As I started to leave, she walks with me to the outside door to show me, she is growing two rubber plants and then we walk to a bird feeder which is attached to the outside of her window. She pours a pint of sunflower seed in the feeder. She loves to watch the birds, they are part of her entertainment, and she feeds them everyday. She was born 1894 in Big Cataloochee, lived there until 1920. She was remarkable to be 102 years of age. (Now deceased)

This is where Ethel grew up.

Creek George Palmer's house and family
Davidson Gap

John Palmer Home Place under Ball Top,
Davidson Branch Cataloochee, NC

This photo taken several years after the Park took over. Photo – GSMNP *Melt down*

William Hamilton Jarrett and Harriett Palmer Jarrett
Cira. 1888
Photo courtesy of two Cataloochee descendants: Gary Stamey. Carlano, Texas and Chris Cirrincione, Chicago, Ill.

Harriett Palmer 1863-1901.
Daughter of George Lafayette and Mary Jane Caldwell Palmer.
Photo courtesy of: Garey Stamey, Carlano, Texas, and Chris Cirrinclone, Chicago, Ill.

Cora (Burgess) Leatherwood

Cora Burgess married Jan. 22, 1927 to Hiram Leatherwood (9/4/1906-5/6/1977). Cora celebrated her 89th birthday July 20, 1997 she was born in Cataloochee. She was the granddaughter of Harriett Caldwell Cook and Daniel Cook. Photo courtesy of: Lucille Bryson.

Palmer's Loan Money

George Fayte and his brother Jessie Palmer were careful about their financial matters, e.g.: In Haywood County there are Deed Books, there are Chattel Mortgages which were executed in secure debts which were owed them 21 March 1877 Sarah (Sally) Hannah on debt to Jessie Palmer for sum of $15.00 due by security to Sarah Hannar on medical account in favor of D.H.M. Rogers and to secure payment of the same. I Sarah Hannah do hereby convey to him these articles of personal property (to wit) one read (red) cow, about twelve years old, one sow black and white shoted with six pigs, but on this special trust, that if I fale to pay said debt on or before the 1st day of October A.D. 1877 they he may sell said property or so much there of as may be necessary, by public auction for cash first giving twenty days notice at three public places, and apply the proceeds of such sale to the discharge of said debt and interest on the same and pay any surplus to me. Deed Book N. p. 51. Source: Dr. Carroll Research for Historic Structures Report Little Cataloochee, N.C.

Bonnie Childers Caldwell and husband, Jarvis Caldwell
Photo: Courtesy of Raymond Caldwell

Samuel and Sarah Cook Hall (Daughter of Daniel and Harriett Colwell Cook

Photo Courtesy of: Beatrice Sisk.

Daughters of Jim & Avie (McElroy) Caldwell - R. Blye Caldwell & (L) Eula Caldwell Underwood at the Big Cataloochee reunion.

at 2001 reunion - Dr. Houck Medford & wife making music with Lowell (L) and Harold Hannah (R)

Joseph & Josephine (Howell) Noland
Parents of Eleanor Noland Palmer (wife of William Hiram Palmer who was a son of "Fate" Palmer).
Print donated by Mrs. Eunave Palmer Perkins

Archibald Bennett & Mary Sisk Bennett
Photo courtesy: Roger Ford
Grassy Fork, Hartford, Tn.

Gas truck - Carter Matney Smathers (L) and Floyd Woody (R)

Edward A. and wife Eliza
(Caldwell Grooms) Leatherwood
Photo: Courtesy of Lucille Bryson.

Myrtle and Pearl Garrett

L to R *Eulala Palmer Caldwell, Pearl Valentine Caldwell And Grandma, Lizzie Howell Caldwell.*

Tommy and Eldridge Caldwell, Sam Killian, Thad and Lloyd Caldwell going to pull car out of lake for Alexander's, who had a ranch in Cataloochee about 1933.

Tine & Elizabeth Bennett

Eston Caldwell and Grady Burress
Eston is the son of Dr. Caldwell

William H. and Eleanor Noland Palmer
Photo Donated by: Mrs. Eunave Palmer Perkins

L to R Mary Medford Caldwell, her husband, Hardy Caldwell, Minnie Caldwell Davis, her husband, Thurman Davis, Eller (Ella) and Tommy holding baby Jack and Betty Caldwell top of steps Dock and Cora and Annie Caldwell. 1934

On Right: Hattie Caldwell Campbell with child. Her Son-in-Law Ernest Edwards, her daughter, Elizabeth Howell Caldwell and Verlin Campbell husband of Hattie. Photo: Courtesy of Florence Evans.

Vaughn Palmer and Ruth Smathers, Teacher lived at William Palmer's house.
Photo courtesy of Doug Smathers

Jim Caldwell and mule

Jim Caldwell looks happy riding his mule and smoking his pipe.

George Ira Washington McGee's Family

Front row: Clara Lucille (Moore) Davis, Hettie Ester (McGee) Moore, Mary Ruth (Moore) McMahan, Sara Jane (Henry) McGee, Dwight McGee, Silas Andrew McGee, Grant Oliver McGee, Sarah (Messer) McGee, George Ira Washington McGee

Back Row: Chester or Jess Raby, William Claude Caldwell, Gazzie (McGee) Caldwell

The Hall place, which was below the iron bridge.
Preacher is 6th from left.
Photo courtesy of Hershel Caldwell

Jonah Brown and wife Sychin Coggins
Photo courtesy of Dora Brown Warren

Benjamin Parker Hopkins

Photo: Courtesy of Roger Ford, Grassy Fork, TN.

Benjamin had twelve sons, who fought in the Civil War, some fought for the Confederates, some for the Union. To read more about them, see *"Civil War Letters and Memories from the Great Smoky Mountains"* by this author.

Benjamin Parker Hopkins born Dec. 4, 1808. Died Nov. 28, 1884. Married Ruth Tinker Nov. 23, 1826.

Benjamin Parker Hopkins was authorized in 1845 by the State of Tennessee to open Cataloochee Turnpike. He also served as school board member in Cataloochee.

Left: Tine Woody and Right: Jack Woody
Sons of Sherman Woody, lived on Little Cataloochee

Tine had on little shoes made from a man's felt hat.

Eldridge and Pearl Caldwell taken about 1950

Left to right: Mark, Mont, Robert and Fred Hannah. They have all brought food to the Cataloochee reunion

Mark Hannah and wife Verdie, on left is Joyce, behind her is Lois. The tallest boy is Harold and Lowell in front.

These are Will Messer's Daughters

Vera Valerie Eula

Ollie, Verda and Ola daughters of Will Messer

Alice Hall and 2 Hannah girls.

Laura Bennett Ford, Daughter of Archibald and Mary Sisk Bennett
Photo courtesy of:
Roger Ford

Mary Ann Palmer wife of Turner Bennett.
Photo courtesy: Roger Ford, Grassy Fork, TN.

Charles Ray Caldwell's Barn
Built by Uncle Andy Caldwell
3/2/1940 photo. Melt down.

Uncle Tine Woody Who lived on Little Cataloochee
Copied from old photograph loaned by Milia Valentine Woody. Photographer: H.C. Wilburn 5/11/1937

Helen and Lillian Hannah
Daughters of Mark Hannah. This Photo was made when their father, Mark was Park Ranger.
Donated photograph

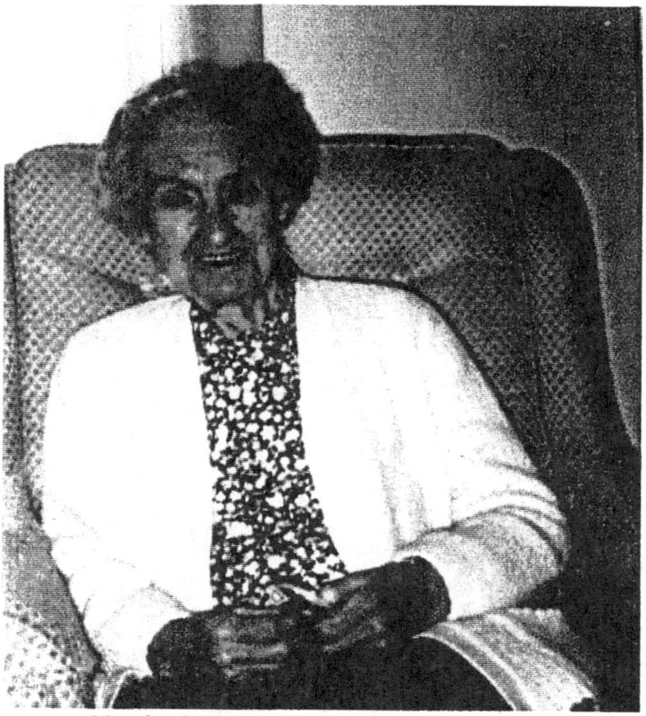

Verdie Messer Hannah wife of Mark

Mark Hannah at Park Ranger station after the Park took over. He was Park Ranger for 31 years.

Wade 1938-'39
Photo courtesy of Wade Caldwell

Big Cataloochee Reunion about 1938

Little boy in foreground is Wade Caldwell, son of Guy, grandson of the second Levi.

Notice of some of the men wearing hats and coats and several women wearing hats and none wearing slacks. The homemade tables extended around the front of the church (Palmer Chapel). You can see Nellie Ridge and a portion of it cleared for grazing, across the creek. Today there are trees grown up along the old road in front of the church, you can't see this portion, of course there are trees grown everywhere and it looks like one great forest, which it is.

Pap Levi and Wade Caldwell

Levi Caldwell - son of Harrison, grandson of the 1st Levi in Cataloochee, with his grandson Wade Caldwell, son of Guy. Levi was called Pap by his grandchildren.

Uncle Harrison

William Jarvis Harrison Caldwell (Colwell) born Feb. 9, 1844 son of 1st Levi in Cataloochee. See page 290 in *Reflections of Cataloochee.* Photo Courtesy of Wade Caldwell

This rainbow was 19 inches long!

Ethan Evans

The Largest brown trout he caught was 24-inches long

Of course there are plenty of stories about the big ones, but see the photos of the big ones that didn't get away from Ethan Evans. He was born and raised on Caldwell Fork, he fished there all his life. Now that he has retired he goes fishing often.

Fishing

Cataloochee has always been known for good fishing. In the early days they say the creeks were so full of the native speckled trout that there was hardly room for them to swim. Gudger Palmer remembered when the rainbow trout were brought in, they were called California trout, later the streams were stocked with brown trout, and he says they are taking over or over crowding the creeks. He says now the little speckled trout are in very high remote areas, where the larger fish cannot travel, and they are very scarce.

There was always a big platter of fish on the table at our house anytime anyone went fishing. The men taking their cattle out to pasture on some grassy bald in the springtime always took a frying pan and necessary items to catch and cook fish. They said they preferred the smaller ones, five or six inches long and ate them bones and all (bones were soft at that stage) a good source of calcium.

Descendants

There are so many Caldwells, Colwells and various spellings over the years it is difficult to know which ones are your relatives. The first in Cataloochee spelled their name Colwell, which is on their headstones, yet the next generations spelled it Caldwell, of course there were no public schools until 1838 and much later in Catalooche. We think the census takers spelled the name like it sounded to them. Then we read that there were the Scotch Irish set of Caldwells of which we are descendants. Also a group of French Hugnots by the same name.

Lloyd Caldwell, son of Tommie and Ella said, "The Caldwells had been on Big Cataloochee several years, then there was a man named Dick Caldwell who settled on Hemphill with his family. Then another set of Caldwells came to live in Waynesville. In order to know which group they were speaking of, they labeled them as the Cataloochee Caldwells, the Dicks and Esaws, which is a Biblical name, no one we can find who knows how that came about. At the time (about 1880) they could not find that any of the three groups were related. Records were not easily available then as they are now, probably no one had done research in recent years, except Dr. Roy Carroll who researched the first and second generation of Caldwells in Big Cataloochee for the Historic Structures Report that he did. It can be found in *"Reflections of Cataloochee Valley"*.

The Mormons in Salt Lake, Utah wrote for permission to use the genealogy, in which we were happy to give it to them, it may help fill in a missing link.

We will never run out of Cataloochee descendants: Most families were large in the early days. If I have counted correctly, Levi and Mary Ann Colwell (Granny Pop) had 12 children and lost one and had 83 grandchildren.

Son Harrison had 10 lost 1

Andy had 6 and lost 2

Marion had 9 and lost 1

Hiram had 5 and lost 1

John had 2 and lost ?

Doctor had 7 and lost 0

George had 8 and lost 0

Reuben had 10 lost 0

Daughter Harriett had 10 lost 0 (2 no birth certificate in N.C. they were probably born in California.)

Matilda had 4 and lost 0

Nancy Jane had 12 and lost 0

See Appendix *Reflections of Cataloochee Valley.* Can you imagine 83 grandchildren! We are not sure about the number of children that Rueben had because he had 2 wives.

Three of Harriett's daughters, Hester who married John Burgess, Rachel who married Will Messer and Sarah who married Samuel Hall, all had 11 children each and one son Riley, married three times and had 26 children, that makes 59 great grandchildren from just 4 of the grandchildren and we know there were lots and lots more. It would be interesting if someone could finish counting, but this is enough to prove my statement, that we will never run out of Cataloochee Descendants!

Cataloochee Descendants

Genealogical information of the first two generations of Caldwells to live in Cataloochee by Dr. Roy Carroll can be found in *"Reflections of Cataloochee Valley."* He said this genealogy needs to be completed. I hope someone will. Dr. Carroll advised to be careful to note your source of information, if it is from a family bible, marriage licenses, a birth certificate, death certificates, a headstone or land records it is very important to note where you got your information as well as all dates etc. These first two generations of Caldwells married into 26 different sir names, they are: Bennett, Brooks, Bryson, Burress, Cagle, Campbell, Childers, Cook, Davis, Evans, Hall, Howell, King, Leatherwood, McElory, McGee, Mooney, Moody, Naillon, Owens, Palmer, Rich, Sutton, Valentine, White and Woody.

Eldridge Caldwell, father of this writer, son of Hiram, Grandson of the 1st Levi Colwell in Cataloochee. Photo made by his grandson Philip Caldwell

About 1987 On the front porch of the Caldwell house.
The house this writer was born in.
My Mother, Pearl Caldwell, Hattie (this writer) her son,
Gil Grasty and his daughter, Monica.
Four generations of the Caldwell family.

Many people can trace their linage back to Cataloochee not only these listed above, because that is just one family spread out. There were many other sir names, with large families.

These Are Post Offices in USA		ZIP
Alabama	Caldwell	351-46
Alabama	Colwell	359-05
Arkansas	Caldwell	723-2
Georgia	Caldwell	31009
Georgia	Colwell	305-04
Idaho	Caldwell	36-05
Ill	Caldwell	619-11
Iowa	Colwell	506-20
Kansas	Caldwell	670-22
New Jersey	Caldwell	070-06
North Carolina	Caldwell	275-72
N.C. Caldwells	Mecklenberg Co.	280-78
Ohio	Caldwell	437-24
Pennsylvania	Caldwell	177-45
Tennessee	Coldwell	371-83
Texas	Caldwell	778-36
West VA	Caldwell	249-25

We wonder how many Colwells, Caldwells, came to America in the early years, how many are related? Most are Scotch-Irish but I have heard some named Caldwell were French Huganots.

Vernon J. Palmer, Son of Will Palmer,
Feed chickens at their home in Cataloochee.
(1930) Print donated by: Eunave Perkins
who is seen at left.

Left to right: Flora Burress Caldwell, Marshal, Juanita and Homer Caldwell (Homer son of Uncle George) dog, Ted. Photo courtesy of: Linda Fulbright Rathbone

Flora Burress Caldwell on r. her sister, Julie Burress on l. Children, Marshal and Juanita sitting on a chicken coop.

Doc Burress wearing his medals from the Spanish American War of 1812. His wife Mattie Lockman Burress, their son Pink between them grandchildren on their lap, Juanita and Marshal Caldwell.
Photo Courtesy of Linda Fulbright.

Juanita and Marshall Caldwell feed the chickens out by the chicken coop on Shanty Branch.

Photo courtesy of: Linda Fulbright Rathbone

Marshall and Juanita Coldwell. Shanty Branch

Photo courtesy of: Linda Fulbright

Boys will be boys! Marshal rides his dog.
See the rock wall and nice fence. Uncle George place
Shanty Branch.
Photo courtesy of: Linda Fulbright Rathbone

Hub Caldwell
Son of Uncle Marion
Grandson of Levi

Maude Lee Caldwell
Wife of Hub
Photos: Courtesy of Gilmer Caldwell

Beech Grove School

Mildred Deal Thompson

A letter from Mildred Deal Thompson dated November 19, 1997. She says I taught in Big Cataloochee for three years. My first year was 1949-50 term. I usually had four grades and seven students. In some cases it was one student per grade.

National Geographic had a picture and a very short write-up October 1952 issue.

One day I had a second grade boy tell me that I was keeping them too long, I looked at my watch and saw that I wasn't, I told him it wasn't time to go. He said, "I know it is because we go when the sun is on this plank and you have let it get all the way over to here. Note: Her students were the children of Park personnel, all others had moved away long before 1949. She was Mildred Deal from Franklin, N.C.

An interview with Mrs. Ruth Smathers July 1999. She remembered when she was offered a job teaching at Cataloochee in early 20s. She was just out of college. Her daddy and mother decided they would take her over there and find out just what kind of people she would be dealing with.

Her daddy drove an old Essex car by the time they got there; she had gotten sick from the fumes from the old car. She was embarrassed but soon got over it.

She was to board at William Palmers house and her parents were pleased when they met the Palmers and others. She remembered Mr. Palmer had lots of cattle and was gone lots of time. The Palmers had a piano in the parlor, which she played and at church she played the organ.

She said the children were well behaved and never gave her any trouble, she couldn't remember whipping any students. She had fun playing ball with the children, but they could out run her.

She remembered one Sunday she and Burr and Blye Caldwell rode horseback to a revival at Little Cataloochee, some young men went along too. She was courting Vaughn Palmer and so was Magola Caldwell, in the photo you will notice she had on silk stockings, they all turned out to be good friends.

Magola Caldwell and Ruth Smathers

Ruth's parents had met my grandparents and been invited to eat with them and all the people really respected a school teacher and were so friendly that her parents decided it was a good place for her to start teaching.

Another Little Cataloochee School teacher in a letter Mrs. Gay Bennett Teague said she taught school at Little Cataloochee in 1926-27 and that her mother taught at Big Cataloochee before then. Gay was living in

Franklin at the time she wrote. She had a desire to get back to Little Cataloochee for the homecoming.

Both Mont and Fred Hannah were teachers at Little Cataloochee and so was Flora Messer.

Palmer remembers when the sheriff still rode horseback

Sometime between 1909 and 1911, when William Palmer was sheriff of Haywood County, word came that a lynch mob was gathering.

The mob was after a man, a Cherokee Indian accused of attacking a woman then hiding out in the Balsam area.

When emergencies arose, the sheriff usually rode out on Big Mac, his black horse. But this time Palmer enlisted the help of a local doctor, one of the few in Waynesville who owned a car, and the two headed for Balsam.

Gudger Palmer, William's son, was a small child, less than 10, when his father raced the lynch mob, but he remembers the story well.

"My father got the doctor to take him up there, and they found the Indian and brought him back," Gudger Palmer remembered.

"The mob had the road blocked somewhere on the way, but they ran around the blockade. The crowd started chasing them, and they were running pretty fast, and this Indian's hat blew off.

"He wanted to stop and get his hat (they didn't) but they got him in safely," Gudger said.

Gudger Palmer was only 2 when his father was elected sheriff of Haywood County and the family moved from the mountain valley of Cataloochee into town into the county jail.

William Palmer and his horse, Big Mac

Milia Palmer did the cooking for the prisoners at the county jail.

He would spend much of his childhood at the jail below the old courthouse on Montgomery Street. The sheriff's quarters were in the front section of the building, and prisoners were housed in the back.

Despite the lynch mob and a few other happenings, it wasn't such a bad time to grow up at the jail, Palmer said. Most of the time life was peaceful, the crimes petty, and the prisoners nonviolent.

He grew up in a day when town and country came together, when boundaries between urban and rural life were sketchy at best.

Take their street, Montgomery Street. Though it was directly below the courthouse and Main Street, Montgomery was a dirt road, with a sidewalk made of planks running along beside. On one end was a blacksmith's forge; a tin shop was at the other.

Across the street from the jail was a pasture, where the sheriff kept his milking cow and the big black horse. There was also a barn, where the family kept feed for the horses and a buggy.

In the mornings, after milking, "we would drive our cow out Montgomery Street, up Depot Street and up Main Street by the courthouse, and out to east Waynesville for pasture," Palmer remembered. "And we'd go get her late in the day and drive her back by the courthouse, back to the barn."

Three or four prisoners usually stayed in the jail, but sometimes the number rise to eight or 10, Palmer remembered. In some ways, Milia (pronounced Mylee) Palmer, William's wife, became as responsible for the prisoners as her husband.

"My mother did the cooking, and all you were required by law to give the prisoners was bread and water," Gudger said. "But she gave them a good meal, plenty of food." Milia Palmer did more than just cook.

"In the outer part of the jail, there was a big room, and quite often if the cells were full or if a prisoners was one who had just a minor case, we would keep him in the outer room," Palmer said. "One day, while my mother was carrying food in, she went back into the kitchen to get more food and left the door open. She glanced back over her shoulder and saw one of the prisoners going out the side door.

"So she followed him on up there to Main Street, about where the old library was... and cornered him up there and talked him into coming back to jail.

"The prisoners occasionally would have a breakout," he said. "We kept the prisoners in cells with iron bars, but occasionally somebody would slip in a file and they'd file out the bars enough to crawl out. Once they were out of the cell, the jail's outside walls were made of brick, so they could scratch the brick enough to get it loose and climb out."

But neither prison escapees nor running the barricade could compare to the excitement generated by the arrest of Nance Dude, Palmer said.

Nance Dude, an old woman from a poverty-stricken family, was charged with murdering one of her grandchildren by taking the toddler in a cave and covering the front with rocks, leaving the child to die.

"My father was sheriff at the time," Palmer said. "He was in on the hunt when this child was reported missing. They finally found him in the cave there out just beyond Dellwood. So they accused Nance Dude of putting the child in the cave and putting big rocks in front so it would starve to death, but she never did own up to it.

"While she was in jail there, my father got word one night there was a lynch mob forming at Depot that was coming up to get Nance Dude. So he hid the keys to the jail in the fireplace chimney in the living room, but luckily that lynch mob never did come.

"She didn't look real well, and her hair was always stringy," Palmer remembered. "She would hardly talk any more than she had to."

Neither Palmer nor his parents ever knew or tried to conclude whether Nance Dude committed the crime that so shook Haywood County. But a jury did convict her, and she was given a life sentence to be served at the state prison for women in Raleigh.

"My mother and Barry Plott, who was a deputy for my father took Nance Dude to Raleigh to the prison on the train," Palmer said. "Going down my mother said Nance Dude wouldn't get over two feet away from her, she was so afraid something would happen to her.

"When my mother started to leave, she said, 'Nance, I want you to tell me the truth; are you the one who put that child in the cave?' And she said Nance looked me straight in the eye and said, 'I am just as innocent as you are.'"

Nance Dude would be paroled after many years and live to be well over 100.

William Palmer always intended to return to Cataloochee, Gudger said, and after the sheriff's third term, he decided not to run again. So after spending another year in Waynesville so the sheriff could finish up tax collection work, the Palmers returned to their mountain valley with the cow and Big Mac.

The big black horse had been part of Sheriff Palmer's career from the beginning, Gudger said. His father campaigned on the mount, and some folks said the two made an impressive scene.

The three elections for sheriff were close, Gudger Palmer said, particularly the first one. The week of the election, William Palmer was in town, but Milia was back on Cataloochee.

"We had no telephone, and my mother back home was anxious to know whether he got elected or not," Palmer said. "My father had told her that if he didn't get elected he was going to trade Big Mac.

"So she kept watching. Our house was on a hill overlooking the road and the next day or the second day after the election she finally saw him coming around the curve, and he was on Big Mac.[1]

---

[1] Monday August 24th 1992 *Growing up at the county jail* by Kathy N. Ross News Editor ***The Waynesville Mountaineer***.

Chapter 7

Ola Baptist Church, Little Cataloochee.
Built 1880

Will Messer made this beautiful woodwork.

The church is one of three buildings still standing in Little Cataloochee. 2002

Buildings that were in Cataloochee before the Park

The building pictured here are not all of the buildings that were in Cataloochee, others are in *"Reflections of Cataloochee"* and there may still be others in the Park archives in Gatlinburg or in family photographs.

There are only three buildings remaining in Little Cataloochee 2 log cabins and the church and in Big Cataloochee there are four houses, two barns, three springhouses and the church and the school.

There are no buildings remaining on Caldwell Fork.

Jessie McGee - smokehouse Caldwell Fork

See the perfect dove tail notches where the corners are fitted together. See the once neat picket fence? Melt down. Photo courtesy: GSMNP

Jim Caldwell House - long after they had to leave

Rough Fork, Cataloochee, N.C.
11/30/1937

Meltdown

Turkey George Palmer barn
Pretty Hollow Creek, Cataloochee, N.C.
Photo: GSMNP
Melt down.

Jim Evan's Cabin
Caldwell Fork, Cataloochee, N.C.
12/3/1938.
Photo: GSMNP
Melt down.

Tynt Woody Big House
Mossy Branch, Cataloochee NC
Photographer: E.E. Extine 4/22/1937

John Jackson Cabin. Photo by Hattie

The John Jackson Hannah Cabin in Little Cataloochee stands in a clearing on a gentle slope. The yard was once enclosed by a rail fence. In the south corner of the front yard were bee gums. Beyond the fence was a vegetable garden; there was also an apple orchard. To the north, west, and south were three cultivated fields.

The out buildings were a springhouse 135 feet northeast and a corn crib with shed 185 ft. north of cabin and a privy, it's location unknown.

Today these out buildings are all gone. The orchard, garden and fields are all gone. The fields are now wooded.

The log house is roughly 22 x 18 ft. it is a one-story structure with a full sleeping loft. The peak of the roof is 19-feet above ground level. It has stairs to the loft and you can see where there was a railing around the opening of the stairs, as a general rule all the children slept upstairs, parents downstairs. This house has a red brick fireplace with a Roman arch and a tall brick chimney.

It is a representative of the better type log structures found in Haywood Co. N.C. (and there were many well built in the Cataloochee area). John Jackson Hannah built this house between 1857-1864, using native stone and timer, hemlock, poplar, chestnut, locust and tiz wood.

The cabin originally had split-board window closures, later replaced with glazed sashes. An addition to the house was called an ell and back porch were added, the ell was a room on the back of the house was used as a kitchen. There is still some forsythia growing as a witness of the past among the briars and bushes, which have covered much of the area.

This structure is one of the few remaining log houses illustrative of the social, cultural, and economic history of the region. It has two distinguishing features: the puncheon floors 4 to 5-inches thick, some of which are 29in. wide: and the chimney of handmade red brick which was rare in this area.

The bricks were handmade, burnt in the field above the house. The mud was mixed by tramping with the feet, then packed into sanded molds, then turned out on a flat surface. A fire was built inside a kiln. It took 7 days to burn one kiln.

Much of this old house was deteriorating and was restored by the Great Smoky Mountain National Park Service back in the 70's. Now it badly needs new shingles on the roof, many of them look almost like fiber strings.[1]

The rock hearth in front of the fireplace, is falling, may be due to hogs rooting under the house. June 2002, there was plenty of evidence that the hogs were in Little Cataloochee, rooting in all the ditches and damp places.

---

[1] Dr. Roy Carroll's research in part. Historic Structures Report. Little Cataloochee, N.C.

John Jackson Hannah House

Bob Caldwell of WLOS 2002 TV

Hand made brick chimney, and window replacement being inspected by Bob Caldwell of WLOS TV 2002 - Photo by Hattie.

Roman arch fireplace made of homemade brick in this John Jackson Hannah cabin

Photo June 2002 by Hattie

James A. and Melissa Hannah, October 1935.
G.S.M.N.P. Photo
Were the last to live in this house.

James A. Hannah (Jim) born 1871 earned a living farming, cutting timber for sawmills served as Justice of the Peace and taught Sunday School Class in Little Cataloochee. He carried mail between Big and Little

Cataloochee. He was a large man, slightly over 6-ft. tall, he was called Uncle Jim by everyone.

In 1893 John Jackson transferred his land and home place to James A. Hannah and wife M.A. (Melissa) during their lifetime.

He married Margaret Melissa Coggins December 1883, she was from Cosby, Tennessee, and they had five children. They were the last family to live there.

This is a photograph of the John Jackson Hannah house long after the Hannah's had to leave, it shows there was a kitchen on the back.
Photo: GSMNP

This shows how solid the house was constructed, this is the interior, which had been papered, probably with newspaper or catalogues - at any rate it would serve as insulation and make the room lighter. There were only two windows, one on each side of the fireplace.

Upstairs was the sleeping loft, it still has wooden shutters that could be opened or closed.

Photo showing some open fields and pasture land in Little Cataloochee, about 1938. This is Coggins Branch looking southwest from the Baptist Church. Most of the people had left and the fields had started growing up. Photo courtesy of GSMNP

William A. Palmer barns

Melt down. *Photo: GSMNP*

Part of Eldridge Caldwell farm before 1934

He moved his family, farm equipment, livestock and other things in March 1934 to Maggie Valley and many other families moved away that year.

Big Barn, cattle barn, small log house was his sheep barn. This picture was made from his old log house up the road. Donated Photo.

Will Messer's house
Coggins Branch
Little Cataloochee

This house was sold by Park Service, and hauled out, lumber used to build other houses 12/1/37.

He owned 340 acres, some he bought, some his wife, Rachel Cook, had inherited some land, and he farmed, raising corn, cattle, sheep, hogs, and horses. With tenant help he developed highly productive orchards, some years selling $3,000 worth of apples. He also had the only store in Little Cataloochee and the post office; he named Ola after one of his daughters.

He saved the finest lumber and made coffins, his wife lined them. He sold them for $7 or if a family could not pay, he gave them free of charge. The Messer's had 11 children. They had built a beautiful log cabin when they first married, later when they were so well established they decided to build a large house, Mr.

Messer (and probably Mrs. Messer) went to see the new Hiram Caldwell house on Big Cataloochee (with blue trim), Hiram was her uncle. They liked the house and Mr. Messer decided to build one just like it except larger, which he did.

Will and Rachel (Cook) Messer
Rachel was the Daughter of Daniel & Harriet (Colwell) Cook

Photo courtesy of: Mark and Verdie Hannah

The people in Little Cataloochee as they were also in Big Cataloochee, were happy and contented living in a peaceful free world of their own, then the Park Service evicted them, to let all their hard work of clearing fields grow up into briars, brush, bushes and trees. The awful heartache of having to leave their homes, then return for the reunion to see the houses slowly deteriorate and fall down. Many tears were shed, but they said they would never give up Cataloochee, and now 70 years later we have not given up the pleasure of going there to day dream and reminiscence, a few never did return.

Mr. Messer finally accepted the $35,405 offered him in a condemnation settlement. He was very bitter, he declared he had the best place in Cataloochee, but received "no more than half the value." "I have tried it out and I find I couldn't buy that sort of place for double the money. With fences and grass and everything, I was robbed out of $35,000 clear dollars."

He finally had to accept the offer and move on. He purchased 1,208 in Caldwell Co. in Happy Valley. For the rest of his live he continued to farm and operate a general store. Mr. Messer always enjoyed working; on

Dec. 4, 1946 he was found dead in his corncrib where he had been preparing feed for his cows. His widow, Rachel, died Aug. 4, 1964.

Mrs. Louise Liner who had worked many years ago in the early 20's with Haywood County Welfare, talked about going to Cataloochee camping out and having fun. I inquired what was it like then, she replied, "oh, honey, most of the people were thought of as the well-to-do, lots of big homes and farms and they certainly ate well. They were such friendly people always invited visitors to eat with them or to stay with them."

She said, " of course there were a few exceptions I found that mostly those who came in late after all the best land was taken. All they could get was some steep rough land, hard to farm but they managed to make a living."

"I was sent to check on them, they didn't have much but they were happy people, they never asked for any aid from the county, they were a proud people."

Jim and Avie McElory Caldwell House. Photo: GSMNP

This is the house Avie McElory Caldwell and Jim Caldwell and family had to leave to the Park in the '30's. Jim's father, Uncle Harrison, son of Levi B. Caldwell in the 1880's, built the house. Jim and Avie both died within a few short years after being forced to leave.

The Park Service did not have the buildings photographed for their archives until many years after the people had to move out of Cataloochee. It is unfortunate the photos were not made when the homes were in their pristine condition.

The main body of this house was of fine log structure. It was done over in yellow poplar; it had two splendid rock chimneys and two beautiful artistic mantles. Footnote: Mr. Wilburn's notes.

There was a large barn out back of this house, Jim's daughters, Ruth and Eula and others had a playhouse in the loft. When we went to visit them, we played up there; we made mud cakes in can lids and had a box for a table. We picked flowers and fixed our table real pretty. Then the boys ran in and messed it up. You bet the race was on.

B. McGaha Can House
Will Palmer Place
Double Branch, Upper Cataloochee
Melted down.

See Photos of other houses in *Reflections of Cataloochee.*

W.G.B. Messer Barn Coggins Branch, Little Cataloochee
Photo: GSMNP

Notice the hay rake on the left side of barn. The long ramp was built for the horses to pull a wagonload of hay or corn into the barn loft.

William Palmer House
Photo courtesy of: Gudger Palmer

Mr. William Palmer was known for his generosity and kindness to those who were less fortunate.

Tommy Caldwell Old Place Chimney
Wash Ridge, Cataloochee, N.C.
12/2/1937 (Melt down.)
Photographer: C.S. Grosman

Gudger and Ottis Hagler, a Baptist preacher.
August 1934

In front yard of the William Palmer house. This house sat on a hill, from there they could see Palmer Chapel, Nellie Post Office, two barns, the large flat meadows, hayfield, haystacks, the public road running along the edge of the meadows. Many say the view from here was unsurpassed. Beyond the meadows flows Cataloochee Creek with speckled and rainbow trout. Gudger Palmer said, "This was truly Heaven's little annex."

See blight damage on American chestnut tree on left.

Home of William and Milia Caldwell Palmer. This house had 8 large rooms; the porch extended around 2 sides. The house had carbide lights. Trunk of trees whitewashed with spent carbide mixture.

The big field below the church called the Mull Meadow, see the hay stacks and rail fence.

Nellie Post Office

Nellie Post Office
Cataloochee, N.C.

Gudger said the sign with the letter "N" backwards was never corrected, Aunt Milia left it as a tribute to an old Indian who made the sign while passing through about the time of the Nellie Post Office was established she thought it was unique. The girl in the center was Hattie Palmer, daughter of William and Milia Palmer. The other two are Mrs. Stockton and daughter visiting from Charlotte, N.C. Incidentally the ladies are not wearing evening gowns. They are big-legged beach pajamas, which they claim to be the casual wear of the day. Considered very fashionable.

In Big Cataloochee closed June 30, 1938 Aunt Milia Palmer was the postmaster and most of the people had moved away and she didn't want to give up her home, but now it would be necessary to move away too. It was a very sad time; she knew it was the end of an era.

When she told her son Gudger that she was going to close the post office, he bought a stamp and an envelope for her to stamp the last letter ever mailed from Cataloochee, the Nellie Post Office. He knew history was being made and he requested this last letter, and has kept it all these many years. (Now 2002)

Envelope postmarked Nellie, N.C. 1938

See postage stamp? (3¢)

Levi Hall Log Cabin, Little Cataloochee, N.C.
Photographer: H.C. Wilburn5/14/1937
GSMNP

Allison Deadin' House
Double Gap Branch of Caldwell Fork Cataloochee, N.C.
Photographer: C.S. Grossman
11/30/1937
GSMNP

This is a team of oxen pulling a sled load of fodder (dried corn stalks and blades) used to feed cattle in wintertime. Photo: GSMNP

This is a shaving horse

Mr. Steve Woody, using a shaving horse. The shaving horse is used to hold a piece of wood while using a drawknife. It is a form of wooden vise: The jaws are brought together by pressure being exerted on a pedal with the foot. He is making hand rived wooden shingles for the roof. Photo: GSMNP

Visitors at George Palmer's house

John Caldwell, J.L. Sutton McGee Branch, Caldwell Fork. 11/29/37. Melt Down.
Photo from G.S.M.N.P.

Jarvis Palmer's Barn Built between 1910-1917.
Big Cataloochee

It still stands.

Mossy Branch, Tine Woody's house
Photo: GSMNP

Hiram Caldwell Springhouse reconstructed
Photo: Hattie

Most young folks never heard of a springhouse. I tell them it's the early refrigerator.

Jarvis Palmer's Blacksmith Shop
Big Cataloochee 12/2/37

Photo: GSMNP

It still stands

Jonah Brown's house on Little Cataloochee
Photo: GSMNP

Melt down

Rhode Hanna's House on Andy Branch
Little Cataloochee
Photo: GSMNP

Melt Down

There are photos of other homes in *"Reflections of Cataloochee."*

Tommy Caldwell barn old place Wash Ridge, Cataloochee, NC
Photo: GSMNP
Melt Down

Tommie Caldwell House and Smokehouse
Wash Ridge, Cataloochee, N.C.
Photo: GSMNP
12/2/37. Melt down.

Old Home Place

Painting of Tommy Caldwell's old home place

Photo shows a painting of the old home place of Tommy Caldwell, daughter Cora remembered the place and remembered moving on a sled, holding her kittens. Cora's grandson Mark Williamson had this painted for her on a rock from the chimney of the old house. It seems that there was great sentiment attached to the fireplace and chimney, so much so a nice flat rock was brought out many years ago. It had been a very sad time when they left the old place moving to Shanty Branch, knowing it would be the very last time they would see it, they chose a special rock for a keepsake, it has the house painted on it.

It would be the perfect symbol to represent the comfort and warmth the fireplace had provided, the wonderful food cooked in big black pots hanging over the fire and where the family laughed and told stories. Yes the rock would be the everlasting symbol of a happy home.

This place was quite a distance back of where Uncle Andy lived (see *Historic Cataloochee Tour Guide* for location) somewhere back there; they say there is a large flat area. It was passed down to me by my father Eldridge Caldwell that is where Levi Colwell and Mr. Young Bennett settled first.

The Large Apple House

Will Messer's Commercial Apple House
Photo 1937 G.S.M.N.P

The large apple house mentioned before, was built by Will Messer in 1915. His wife inherited part of the Cook Farm. The walls of the first floor were native stone. This exceptional thickness was for the purpose of insulation. Historic photographs reveal that the second story walls were chestnut siding 1-in by 10-in. An interview with Mark Hannah, the last man to use the structure revealed that the space between the interior and exterior walls was filled with sawdust for insulation.

The first floor consisted of one room used for grading and packing and for storage of those varieties of apples, which would keep during the winter and be sold later.

This is all that remains of the Will Messer Apple House. Photo - 1975 G.S.M.N.P

This apple house measures 21-ft. 10-in. All of the bins were about 3-ft. 6-in. deep the sides of the bins were little sawmill strips about 1-inch thick spaced 2-in. apart to allow for circulation of air.

Apples had become the major cash crop by 1914. Will Messer designed this building for commercial purposes, to store and ship the 2500 or more bushels of apples annually. The apples were shipped to markets in Charlotte, Gastonia, South Carolina and Knoxville, Tennessee.

There were many orchards in both Big and Little Cataloochee. They were a good money crop and there was no need to use insecticide, because they did not have insects like we do today.

The old time apple trees seemed to be much healthier than the new varieties we have today. The old time apples were Stark Red Delicious, Stark Golden Delicious, Winesaps, Stamens, Jonathans and Black Hoover.

The Burgess Orchard produced 1800 bushels per year. The apples sold for 50¢ to $1.50 per bushel. Some of the apples were sold to the lumber camps at Mt. Sterling, Sunburst, and Crestmont. A portion of the crop was turned into brandy, a neighbor named Braz Whaley had a distillers licenses.[1]

---

[1] Dr. Roy Carroll's Research in Part.

Dedication of the Cook Cabin June 6, 1999

Harold Hannah, descendent of the Cook Family and Karen Wade, Superintendent of the Park. Photo by Hattie

The dedication service began at 1:30 p.m. Karen Wade, superintendent of the Great Smoky Mountains National Park was speaker. She had this to say - The Cook Cabin, built back in the 1800's was one of the oldest and finest examples of a log structure in the Great Smoky Mountains National Park.

The Cook's were a part of a community with a number of other extended families, by the name of Messer, Woody, Bernnetts, Coggins, Brown's, Hannah, Burgess, Conard's, Halls, and Nelsons.

They cleared woodland, farmed, grew grain for bread and livestock, planted apple orchards, wove cloth to make clothing, fished and hunted to feed their families.

The Park was founded in the 1930's the settlers in the Smokies had to abandon their family homes and farms, their church, graveyards and land, and move outside the Park.

The Cook Cabin was still standing in 1975 when vandals damaged it so severely, that Park officials decided to store the remainder of the original material until it could be rebuilt.

Our thanks go to superintendent of The Great Smoky Mountains National Park, and all the rest of Park officials too, for giving us a day of remembrance - when Grandpa Cook's Cabin was once again made new.

Also to Auroa Foods and Log Cabin Syrup too, who provide the funds to build and restore, the Cook Cabin to look almost like it did once before.

Thank you Harold Hannah for being spokesman for the Cook Clan and for carrying on the work which your father "Mark Hannah" once done.

I think it's important, and I believe we will all have to agree - to keep the branches growing from the "Old Family Tree."

Written by Beatrice Sisk

June 27, 1999

Daniel Cook Cabin

Little Cataloochee

The Cook Cabin is in a clearing on level ground, located 72 feet from Davidson Gap or one-half mile south of Little Cataloochee Baptist Church.

It was the earliest and finest log house erected in the area. Daniel Cook built it between 1856 and 1860 using native woods, locust, poplar, hemlock and chestnut and native stone. The quality of the workmanship was a testimony to his skill as a hewer and a carpenter. To the north of the house were open fields, to the south, on both sides of Coggins Branch were open fields, to the south on both sides of Coggins Branch were open fields and apple orchards.

A springhouse constructed of hewn timbers covered by 1x4 inch rived chestnut strips in crisscross lattice fashion. It was eighty feet northwest of the house. A small apple house stood 90 feet to the southwest of the house.

Another stone and lumber apple house, the largest in the region and architecturally and economically one of the most interesting and significant structures in the region stood 166 ft. southeast of the house.

A log barn built by Will Messer 1905 stood 154 ft. southwest of the large apple house. The barn was described in 1935 as two cribs 13x36 ft. with a driveway between the cribs.

The Cook Cabin, facing southeast was roughly 21 feet by about 18 feet. It was a one story with a full loft. The peak was 17-ft.10 in. above the ground; the stone chimney extended 1 foot above that. A porch ran the full length of the house front and back. A portion of the back porch was enclosed for a kitchen area.

The walls were constructed of poplar logs 12 to 18 inches wide and 5 ¾ in thick hewn smooth with chamfer notches at the corners. The flooring was poplar puncheons, 10 inches thick wide random widths.[1]

---

[1] Researched by Dr. Roy Carroll and Raymond Pulley and their field team, Kent R. Cave, Thomas C. Robbins and Norman Schaich.

When the Park Service had this Cook Cabin reconstructed they built the porch around three sides of the house because there were some rock stacks (foundation) on all three sides, they naturally assumed it had front, back and side porches.

Historical research: Joel S. Horton others were, Fred Wilson, Jewel Bentley, Brenda Green, Judith P. Pulley and Evelyn Sheppard.

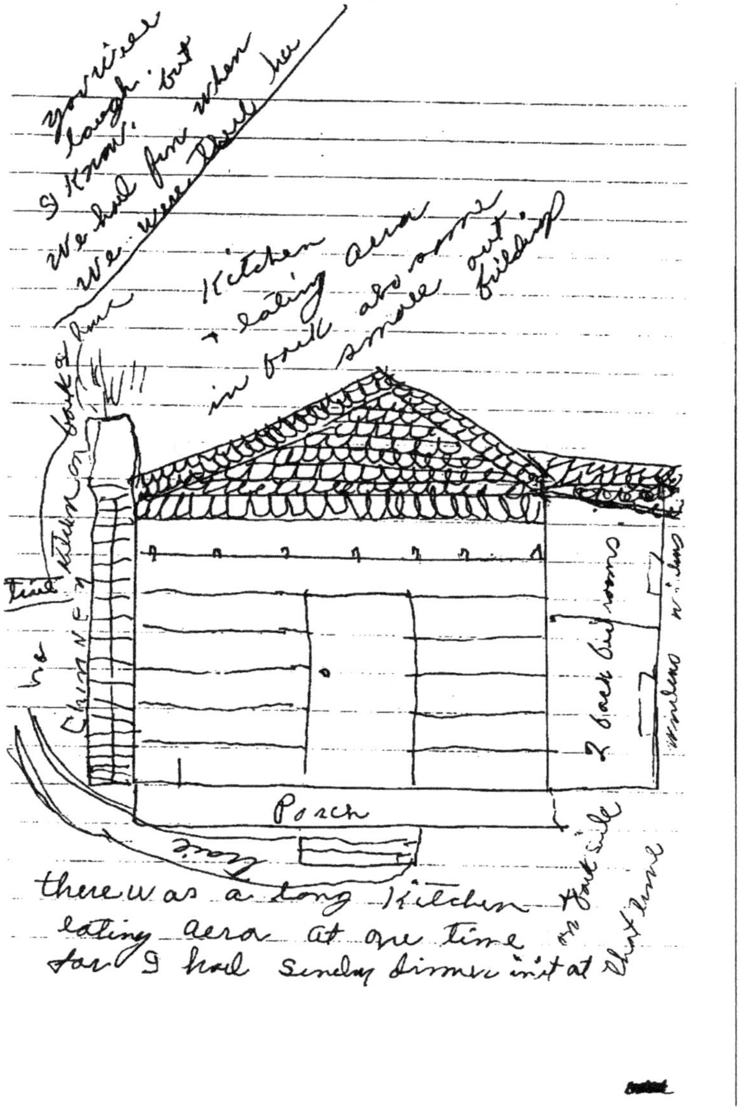

A drawing indicates there were two porches — then two more bedrooms were added - the drawing was from a granddaughter of the Cooks. She was Ola Messer Palmer — in another letter we find a son of the Cooks died as a young married man with children — the Cooks took two grandchildren to raise, which would account for the extra rooms.

We find that an important fact was overlooked when dedication of the Cook Cabin was made that being Daniel Cook's wife was Harriett Elizabeth Caldwell (or Colwell) daughter of Levi Belese and Mary Ann Naillion Colwell.

They were happy with life their family and their neighbors. Most of the people would not have traded their life in Cataloochee for any amount of money, but they were evicted to make way for the Great Smoky Mountain National Park. Today some of the people look back and say its good to have a Park because it will stay the same. That if we had lived there it would have become a resort and over populated.

Its just too bad the Park Service didn't have the foresight to preserve the beautiful log cabins, large homes, the little post office and country store, the corn mills, blacksmith shops and the many barns the rail fences and rock fences. The whole Valley would have been like a complete museum with everything from the beginning to the end of a thriving community 1800s to 1934.

Yes Cataloochee is a place in time where you can go, where time has practically stood still since 1934. You can visit the little white church, Palmer Chapel built 1896, the bell tower was added 1929. They had a church/school before this (see *Reflections of Cataloochee*).

You can see the Palmer house built by George Palmer about 1838-1840. It was originally a two-room dogtrot house (space between the two rooms) about 1865 two rooms were added on the porch and the roof removed then the second story was added. This was done by Fate Palmer who had married Nancy Jane Colwell (daughter of Levi) they had several children and then Fayte's sister, Mary Ann Palmer Noland came home with her children, her husband Allen Noland, had been killed on the way home from the Civil war. See *Civil War* Letters *and Memories by this same author.* Fayte, Mary Ann's brother took on the responsibility of helping her raise her children, he and his wife had a total of 12 children, and it must have been a happy household with so many children there.

About 1881 some of the Cataloochee men took their horses and pulled a water powered portable sawmill up over Cove Creek Mountain then down into Cataloochee Valley. Before that all the structures were made of logs, for the first 50 years everyone lived in a log house, except there could have still been some drovers camps made of puncheons. After the sawmill was brought in, they sawed lots of lumber; several men added more rooms and siding to their log homes. There are only two of this type of house there now the Palmer House, the other one is the Woody House.

The Woody House is a mile or more above the locked gate. Uncle Steve Woody built it. It has two beautiful mantles and fancy wood ceilings. You can tell where the walls are log, look in the doorways and see the thickness of the walls.

Then there were lots of large homes built of sawed lumber; only two of these are standing today. The Hiram Caldwell House.

Granddaddy Hiram Caldwell had the Medford's start building it in 1898 finished 1903, it was definitely hand built, no power tools and no electricity in those days. Their time had to be divided between farming and taking care of large herds of livestock, then building.

The Hub Caldwell house is now the ranger's station it was built 1916. Mr. Wilburn stated it had solid chestnut beams and paneling of chestnut lumber (the blight hit the chestnut trees in 1920's so it's not wormy chestnut).

There are three old barns, the Will Messer barn was moved from Little Cataloochee by the Park Service and reconstructed near the Ranger's house in Big Cataloochee for his horse.

The Palmer barn sits near the Palmer house. It is a nice big barn with a ramp built from the ground up to the barn loft, so they could drive a wagon load of hay up there, unload it, then back the horses and wagon out.

The Caldwell barn sits on the edge of the road across from the Caldwell House. There are four log stalls inside which were hand hewn by Levi Caldwell about 1858, See *Reflections of Cataloochee*.

The schoolhouse and Palmer Chapel are made of sawed lumber. These structures are all that remain in Big Cataloochee. In 1934 when the Park took over there were many large beautiful homes and some of the well constructed log homes, they were kept up in beautiful condition, every one had pride in his family, home, barns and farm lands, it was much like an Amish village.

No log homes were rotting down (as it has been written) until many years after the Park service took over and neglected to keep the roofs repaired. They call it melt down; some large homes were sold for the lumber to build other houses, most were burned by the Park. All were destroyed except the houses that the Park personal lived in, except Uncle Steve Woody's. He and Turkey George Palmer stuck it out in spite of the strict restrictions the Park imposed on people.

The little white school house called Beech Grove built 1906, it is the third and last school built there and where we all went to school through the seventh grade, then the children were boarded out, probably with relatives in other areas to go to other schools. Many of the people moved away 1934.

When I was in school there it was a one-room school, later on when only the children of the Park ranger Mark Hannah and children of the maintenance workers went to school. There were only a few students; a petition was put in to conserve heat. The back room was turned into a place for the children to play when the weather was bad and some coal was stored there to fuel the big pot bellied stove. The school is called Beech Grove School it closed in 1967.

The Park service has a small exhibit and video in the Palmer house (this part was added on by Jarvis Palmer, son of Fayte) in which you can visit.

Mr. Wilburn, surveyor for the Park thought they were going to preserve all the beautiful log cabins, barns and all the homes and make a museum. He collected many antiques and artifacts from the Cataloochee people for a museum. He numbered all the pieces of which I have listed some in *"Reflections of Cataloochee."* We would like to see all those artifacts in a museum before we die.

We have hopes of seeing a museum materialize, now that we have Friends of the Smokies. We all need to talk to them about it. Let them know what we want; they will help if they can. Contributions are needed;

they have made a great improvement in the Park, and its upkeep.

Their address is:

Friends of the Smokies
130 West Bruce St. Suite 1
Sevierville, TN 37862

To see the location of the early homesteads see *Historic Cataloochee Tour Guide,* it also has a map showing the whole area of Big Cataloochee, Little Cataloochee and Caldwell Fork, the names are listed where many of the homes were located also the cemeteries, creeks, branches and mountains.

You would not think so many people lived there when you go there now, but when you look at the map you can get a much better idea of how the area was settled. Dr. Roy Carroll states that the census for 1910 listed 1,251 people living in this area. The *Historic Cataloochee Tour Guide* also has photos of the three remaining structures that are in Little Cataloochee and directions of how to get there.

Little Cataloochee has their reunion in June, some call it Decoration Day, they take flowers for the graves in the cemeteries they have a church service and plenty of good food.

Big Cataloochee Reunion is always in August.

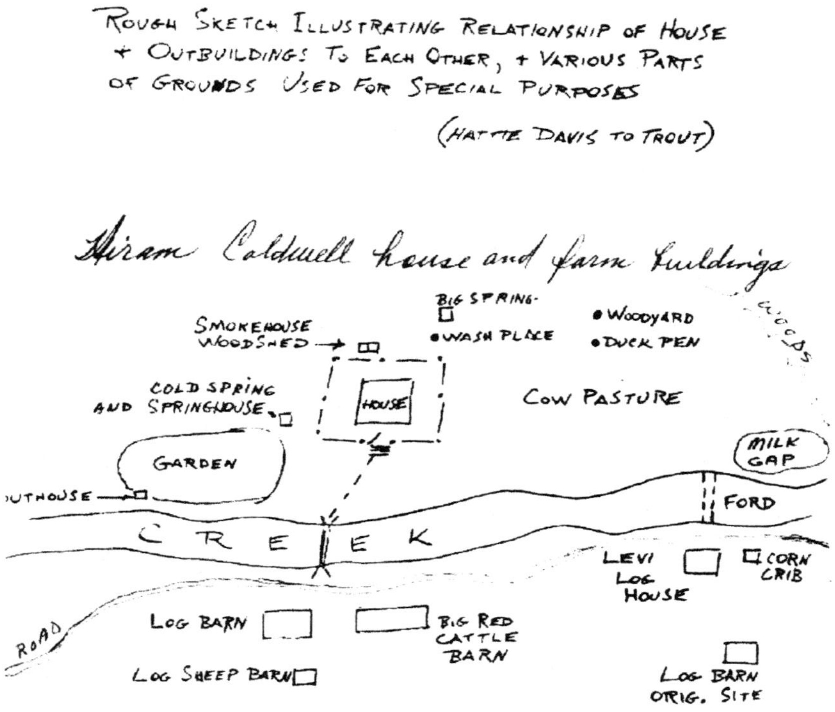

The Hiram Caldwell House

Hiram was the first generation of Caldwells born in Cataloochee in 1851; he was the eighth child of Levi and Mary Ann Naillon Colwell. He was born and grew up in the log cabin, after he married he continued to live there and take care of his mother.

Hiram's house sets across the creek from the big barn, the house sets on a nice little knoll. Hiram must have had his eye on that and dreamed of building his big house there for a long time. He was 42 years old and he was able to pay for it at the time it was completed.

Gudger Palmer said his father, William, told him how they built that big house. Hiram and some men went up on the mountain and marked the finest straight trees, then cut the trees and hooked the horses to them and pulled them to the place where the house was to be built, then they set up the old water powered sawmill. Sawed the lumber to specification, for framing, joist, rafters and all that was needed. The weatherboarding is of yellow poplar all the lumber used was of the finest quality called number one (meaning strong solid wood without knot holes). This is how all the houses were constructed, after the sawmill was brought in.

Hiram bought the brick for the chimney, and the windows and doors in Waynesville and hauled all of that in wagons across the narrow winding road over Cove Creek Mountain he made many trips. Then he hauled the beaded ceiling for the downstairs part of the house, they joked about it being imported from Waynesville.

The road was so rough and rutted out it was always a rough trip; going to Waynesville was referred to as going on a journey. It took one whole day to get a loaded wagon to the top of Cove Creek Mountain, where they would sleep on the ground, if it was raining they slept under the wagon, it gook another whole day to go the rest of the way, it was a four day trip.

Hiram's house is of unusual architectural design having an arch in the hall, the stairs facing the rear entrance and unusual woodwork design of the walls.

The large room upstairs was used for weaving, quilting, storage of food staples and a great place to play, for us kids in the wintertime. The walls in that room of are of hand-planned poplar, which took many days of hard work to make nice and smooth, the walls aged to a beautiful golden patina.

Those walls never had a mark on them when we lived there, now it is a disgrace that the ugly marks are on the beautiful wood, put there by some of the Park visitors, it makes me so sad to see how ugly the marks are.

Those ugly marks show disrespect for the long hard hours of work that went into dressing the boards.

The small room joining the large room had shelves all around the wall; it was used to store canned food. I remember how pretty those glass jars looked all filled up with real yellow and green vegetables. There were some of the older green jars with glass tops and some had zinc tops lined with glass and they need a red rubber ring to seal them.

The exterior of the house was always painted white; it had Williamsburg blue trim (just a couple of shades lighter than navy).

When the Park painted it, they analyzed a paint chip, but it was so old they couldn't get the proper color.

Lush Caldwell and his family were the last to live there. Now the house has been empty since 1967. For a few years the windows were covered with boards and nailed up and the doors were nailed shut. Now it is open to the public.

The trees have grown close to the house, causing it to be dark inside and the wood has turned very dark. Nothing has been done to preserve the interior, it has been hard for the Park to get funds for the new roof, paint, flooring on both porches and many other repairs.

The house is one hundred years old (completed 1903) and will probably be there another hundred years if the Park can manage to keep those wild hogs from rooting the foundation from under this and other historic buildings.

The foundation is made of stacked rock and locust post.

All of those historic buildings in Big and Little Cataloochee should be protected, because they could never be replaced. All of the houses have long histories.

This house is where this writer was born.

Caldwell House 1903

Photo by Hattie

Destruction

The damage to the supports under the Caldwell house were corrected where the wild Russian hogs wallowed out a large bed and left a support post hanging in midair and causing the steps and porch to break loose from the house. We need to pay constant attention to the foundation this house and other historic buildings, because it will most likely happen again.

Damage to the hundred year old Caldwell house

You can plainly see this post is hanging in midair. This was caused by the wild hogs.

Caldwell House, Big Cataloochee

Steps and the back porch breaking loose from the house, because the wild hogs have rooted underneath the support post, there is no support. It will only get worse as many people walk on it. This needs to be repaired quickly as possible; it has been neglected for two years, since I first reported the damage.

This damage was repaired but now 2002, the hogs have rooted the stack of rock supporting the kitchen floor joist causing the kitchen to drop several inches and the porch to break loose again. If this damage is not repaired soon the house will break apart then fall.

The wild hogs are rooting everywhere for food. Daddy's field below the big barn looked like a bulldozer had been at work there and other locations, but it was hogs.

The Park knows the hogs are rooting up trees and all kinds of rare plants and flora but they say they don't have enough manpower to eradicate the thousands of hogs.

When I first found the damage to our house, I went to Gatlinburg and talked to the wildlife officer, he told me they had killed 1,100 hogs, but they multiply so fast they can't ever reduce the numbers.

Perhaps the Park could have an open hunting season on those hogs for one month or even one week each year. The natives here would enjoy the hunt and reduce the hog population quickly; we know it would take an act of Congress to get a law passed for hog hunting.

Hog hunting should be made first priority by the Park in order to save it. Hunting licenses would bring in a good amount of revenue, which the Park needs.

It is always a struggle for them to get enough money to maintain the Park, because there are so many other agencies making request for money.

Legend is that the wild Russian boars were shipped to Graham Co. N.C. by a group of wealthy sportsmen in the 1800s. Members of the hunting club died out, the hogs kept on multiplying, now there are thousands spread out all through the mountains.

We know the Russian hogs are mixed with domestic hogs. John Caldwell lived on Caldwell Fork, when his cow got out (see *reflections of Cataloochee)*, his lease was automatically broken, he had to move, he took his family, furniture and farm tools, then when he came back to round up his hogs (200) the Park said no, all of this is government property and nothing can be removed. What a terrible blow to a hard working man whose family had owned the land for one hundred years. What a hardship and heartbreak it was for the family, that was their main source of income taken from them.

The Park has a few rangers shooting the hogs, but they can't even make a dent because the hogs multiply so fast. Here are the facts when a sow (female) is 5 to 6 months old they will mate the gestation period is only 115-120 days or about four months. They will have two litters or more per year. The litters are usually 10-12 maybe 15 pigs each time. Multiply these numbers and you realize there are probably thousands. The hogs have very few predators.

The Park knows how out numbered they are, but can't afford enough personnel to eradicate the hogs.

The Park now has this great new scientific center on the Purchase Knob, scientist and environmentalist are working to identify these rare plant specimens. It is estimated that there are more than 100,000 unidentified plants. Now (2002) they say they have found 300 plants which have never been found anywhere in the world. It is unknown how many have been completely destroyed by the hogs.

All of the hard work of identifying the plants is a complete waste of time and money, unless the wild hogs are eradicated. It is certain there will be much more destruction if positive action isn't taken and taken soon.

A Primary Mission of the National Park Service is to preserve native plants and native animals on land it manages.

These hogs are NON NATIVE and should not be protected but that is a big bad problem for the Park. The Park personnel say absolutely no hunting is permitted.

There is an alternative that may work. They could do like the old timers who went to gather their hogs from the woods, they made trails of shelled corn; the hogs would eat and follow into a pen.

Perhaps the Park could make trails of corn to the exterior of the Park in some surrounding areas where they could get rid of them.

These are young folks that are carrying on a job that started over seventy years ago. Let's help them keep what's left.

Send tax-deductible contributions to:

Friends of the Smokies

130 West Bruce Street Suite 1

Sevierville, TN 37862

Levi Colwells
second house

Levi's 2nd House 1858

Levi's second house and carriage house with corncrib on one side and harness on the other. Buggies were parked in the middle.

Pen and ink drawing as remembered by great granddaughter Hattie. Drawing by:

Carolyn DeMorest Serrano
PO Box 362
Hendersonville, NC 28793
828-695-3322.

You can contact her for this drawing or any house of your choice on fine board, suitable for framing. Her work looks better than this print. She will make it any size you want.

Levi's 2nd House 1858

In an interview with Mark Hannah (1992) he told me this house had the first closet in any house in Cataloochee, he was fond of my grandfather Hiram who was born there and lived there and when Mark came over from Little Cataloochee to visit he was shown the closet under the stair steps. Ordinarily the clothes would be hung on wooden pegs around the room. Levi must have wanted his house more orderly he built the closet; he also built a large clothespress, six ft. high and sides and shelves are made of one wide board 22 in. wide. It is made of yellow poplar with hand made nails (made by heating a worn out horse or oxen shoe, straightened it out then cut in narrow strips then cut across to proper length.) Thus you have square nails. He surely must have had a blacksmith shop. The boards were hand planed to a nice finish almost smooth.

Hiram moved out of the house in 1903 to his large white house he had built across the creek from the barn.

About 1905 the little Beach Grove schoolhouse happened to burn down. (Not accidentally, see *Reflections of Cataloochee).* Then this log house was used for a school until they got one built. After that the front porch and extra room was removed, the chinking fell out of the cracks and boards were mailed over the cracks to keep out the cold wind and rain, it was used as a blacksmith shop and sometimes to store extra corn or fodder.

Eventually the board shingles gave way and the house was starting to rot down. Eldridge son of Hiram had inherited the farm and house, he had been promised that he could move the log house if he ever moved (it was just a promise to get him to sign the deed.) The Park would not let him move it he was disappointed.

He offered to put new wooden shingles on to protect the house, but no he could not touch it because it was now Government property. I think that was the final straw, that was when he said I will move away before I stay here and watch it rot down, it and all the other houses and when I gather my crops this fall it will be the last farming that I ever do here in Cataloochee.

Cattle barn and storage shed built by Eldridge Caldwell.
This was adjacent to his big barn on edge of road.
Photo in "Reflections of Cataloochee".
Melt down.

Chapter 8

Cataloochee Furniture

Dinning Table

Great granddaddy Levi Colwell (Caldwell) made this table that I wrote about (*Reflections of Cataloochee*). The table and bench are in the museum in Waynesville for every one to see because he was granddaddy, great granddaddy, and great- great and on and on down the line. In fact there are so many descendants we can't count them.

For the tabletop he used three pine boards and home made nails, the legs and base are made of walnut and he used wooden pegs to construct it. The bench was made from a small pine tree, which was split in half, and the legs were pegged in. I grew up sitting on that bench, eating at that table so did many, many others. The table was so long it has been shortened on both ends twice, I guess Levi made it to accommodate his family of 11 children, him, his wife and who ever happened by, they would always ask people to eat with them.

The table was used by Levi and family, after Levi died Jonathan Woody married Levi's widow (Granny Pap) several of her children were still home and he brought 5 of his children, so we know the table was full. Then when Levi's son, Hiram grew up and married, the table was used by his family, after he died Hiram's son Eldridge and his family used the table and still after three generations the old table and bench are just as sturdy as the day they were built. You can go see the table and sit on the bench. You will find it in the Kitchen of the Museum, still called the Shelton House in Waynesville, N.C.

Furniture

Hand made bed and washstand

Just before the Civil War, the Cataloochee turnpike was completed, now people could haul things in or out of Catloochee. Before that a packhorse or mule used to get supplies in, and all of their furniture had been hand made in Cataloochee until then.

There were still no manufacturing plants anywhere near. There were craftsmen who made furniture by hand for sale. Now that they had a road twenty-six years after the first permanent settlers came there, Granny Pop (Mary Ann Naillon Caldwell) ordered two cannon ball beds and a washstand from a Mr. Caton in Catons Grove, Tennessee. The washstand sat beside the bed with a bowl and a large pitcher of water for bathing and a towel hanging on the side also a kerosene lamp and the Bible were on the top.

The washstand and beds are made of poplar wood and not a nail in them, they are totally constructed with wooden pegs and are just as sturdy as if new.

The beds are sometimes referred to as rope beds, because a rope was laced through holes in the sides and ends is such an arrangement as to make 8-inch squares. This was to support the bedding, which was usually straw ticks, or finely shredded shucks in a bed sized bag.

Of course they brought all the furniture from the old log house to the new one and bought more. When we moved, we brought it all to Maggie Valley, most of it was used up stairs in the large house, thank goodness my mother realized the Historic value of it and kept it.

Lot of families had real nice furniture in their homes in Cataloochee, but over the years it was divided among the families and they have moved in all directions in the past 60 or 70 years. I have been able to find and photograph some of it. Photo over the bed is grandpa Hiram and his wife - grandma Lizzie it was their bed.

The beds were quite comfortable especially when a feather bed was added to sleep on at our house we had so many beds, some were of this type but we also had several beds with springs and mattresses when I was growing up. The bed and washstand are still in the family.

Daddy, Eldridge was the youngest of the Hiram Caldwell children and his wife called Aunt Lizzie had lived with and taken care of his mother Granny Pap (Mary Ann Neillon Colwell). After she died Hiram and Lizzie lived on in the log house until he got enough money to build the Caldwell house that still stands in Cataloochee today.

Bed with straw tick mattress

This bed with a straw or shuck tick was photographed in Madison County, 1998. This is similar to beds used in Cataloochee.

Clothes Press

We are not sure how old the clothes press is. We know that great grand daddy Levi Caldwell (Colwell) built it, probably about 1858 when he built the second house.

He used two boards of poplar wood 22-inches wide and 70-inches long these are the sidepieces. The top and bottom and three shelves are all 22-inch wide and 36 inches across. The door has more narrow boards and it still has the original wooden button to keep the door closed.

He must have spent lots of time hand planning the large boards; you still see a few marks of the hand plane. He used some wooden pegs and some homemade nails to construct it. I have been told that when horseshoes were worn out they would be heated red-hot then hammered out straight and cut into strips, then in desired length, that is why the nails are square.

Clothespresses were used in England to store clothes, quilts and other things and used for the same in Cataloochee.

Corner Cabinet

This beautiful cherry corner cabinet was in the old house of Tommy Caldwell, when they moved from the old home place to Shanty Branch, it was hauled on a sled to the Shanty Branch House.

No one in the family knows who made it or how old it is, but we know it is more than 75 years old, because it had been that many years since they moved, Cora said the cabinet was old when she was a little girl.

Hall Tree

This beautiful old oak hall tree stood in the hall on the left side of the Caldwell House in Cataloochee as far back as I can remember, until we had to move. Of course it had been transported there over Cove Creek Mountain on a wagon. When we moved out of

Cataloochee, the hall tree was hauled out in a big truck by Kyle Campbell a nephew of daddy's (Eldridge Caldwell) to the Verlin Campbell house on Campbell Creek Maggie Valley March 1934, where it was in the hall there until 1996.

The hall tree is still in the possession of the family. The loop on the left side is for umbrellas.

Mother (Pearl V. Caldwell) had kept boarders and schoolteachers; she saved her money and bought the hall tree and sideboard in about 1925. Both had been used but well cared for. [1]

---

[1] The mirror does not have a cross on it – don't know how it got in the photo. Photography by Hattie Caldwell Davis.

Sideboard

The old oak sideboard always sat in the dinning room in the Caldwell House in Cataloochee. It was well used, the long drawer in the middle was used to store left over food, like bread, cookies or cake also fried ham or any food that would not spoil until the next meal. Other food was carried to the springhouse that served as a refrigerator; there was a cement trough in which extremely cold water ran through from the spring. The food was place in the water; there was never any worry about food spoiling. The sideboard is still in the possession of the family.

You can see spots on the mirror; these were caused by setting an oil lamp too near the mirror. At night the oil lamps were lit all over the house, usually tow on the big long dinning table and one or two on the sideboard, others in the kitchen and all around.

Cherry table

This table was used on the back porch of our Cataloochee house; it was used to keep a big bucket of cold water for drinking using an aluminum dipper. There was always a wash pan on this table and home made lye soap where everyone washed their hands and face, there was always a towel hanging near by.

You can see groves in the wood, which were made by the lye soap after it was used and the wet soap was laid on the wood. The table was painted white and was always there from my earliest memories.

You would think the lye soap would be hard on their hands, but they had mutton tallow, rendered from sheep the bears had killed. Mutton tallow is a very rich source of lanolin it would soothe their hands very nicely.

Mutton tallow was mixed with beeswax and applied to their shoes, and boots it made them waterproof. Sometimes beef tallow was mixed with beeswax and used to waterproof their shoes too and we wonder if that was used on covered wagon canvas too. We suppose the canvas was homespun and it had to be made to shed the rain.

Daddy's Hair Clippers

Daddy (Eldridge Caldwell) was a good barber; he cut hair almost every Sunday afternoon. This pair of clippers was purchased at the yard sale for 50 cents. We don't know what happened to daddy's original spring-loaded clippers. He quit using them after he bought an electric clipper.

Walnut chest

This sturdy chest of drawers belonged to Cora Burgess Leatherwood. It is made of solid walnut. It was handmade in Little Cataloochee by Will Messer, no one is sure when it was made.

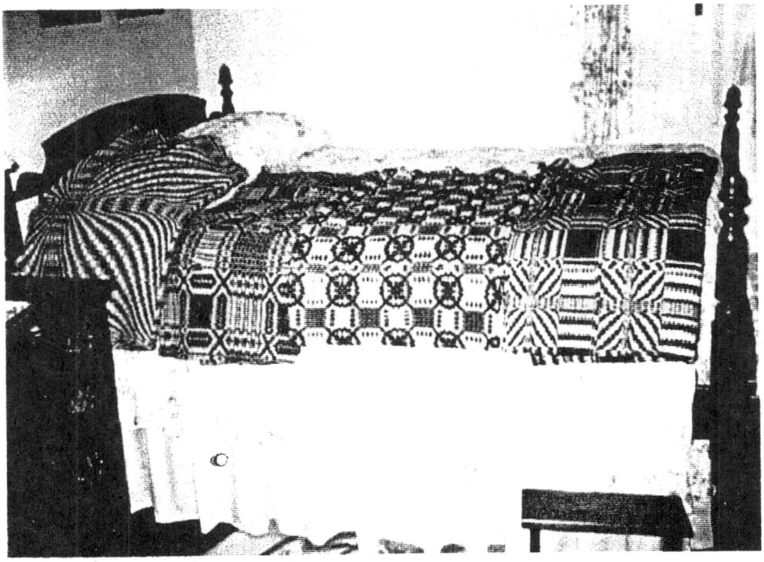

Matilda Colwell married Creighton Bennett, after he died 1870 Tine Woody came to work on her farm, later October 29, 1880 Matilda married Tine. She was said to have been an excellent weaver. These beautiful coverlets were passed down to Mary Dunn, daughter of Sherman (Jim Woody).

Matilda had woven about sixty of these beautiful coverlets; unfortunately all were stolen except eleven.

It took lots of hard work to shear the sheep, wash the wool, card it, spin it into thread, dye it and then weave it into beautiful designs.

The bed made by Daniel Cook

Shows the fine craftsmanship he had. It is put together with wooden pegs. The bed was made some time in the 1800's was used in Little Cataloochee by the Tine Woody family also the Sherman (Jim) Woody family. Now in use by Tine's great granddaughter Mary Dunn.

Round butter dish and square honey dish passed down from Tine Woody Family to Great granddaughter Mary Dunn

Flat irons, tea kettle, pot and churn passed down from the Tine Woody family to his nephew James Sherman (Jim) Woody then to his daughter Mary Dunn.

Mountain Lily Quilt

This quilt was made by Grandma (Mary Elizabeth Howell Caldwell) for her son Eldridge's first baby, Nell, the quilt was made the size of the old time baby beds - larger than today's. One looks at it and has to admire the intricate tiny stitches and the beautiful appliqué work; you look and know it was made with love.

Many of the women in Cataloochee did pride themselves of their fine needlework. They made many beautiful quilts and things.

Old things from Cataloochee

In the floor, a dehorning saw. A stirrup from daddy's old western saddle, an iron teakettle, a churn jar, a well-worn washboard and two hand tied hearth brooms. One-gallon apple vinegar jug.

More old things used in Cataloochee

A flat pan for making pancakes came with 1904 Home Comfort Stove. Old wine jug, 2 flat irons, cow bell, iron shoe last (Could change foot for different size shoes), butter crock, iron pot, copper cowbell, 2 large earthen wear jars in back. These things are sitting under a meal/flour box.

Traps collected in Cataloochee by Mr. Wilburn.

Where are these traps? They should be in a museum. Maybe they are but where? Also many other items collected for a Cataloochee museum. (See *Reflections of Cataloochee*)

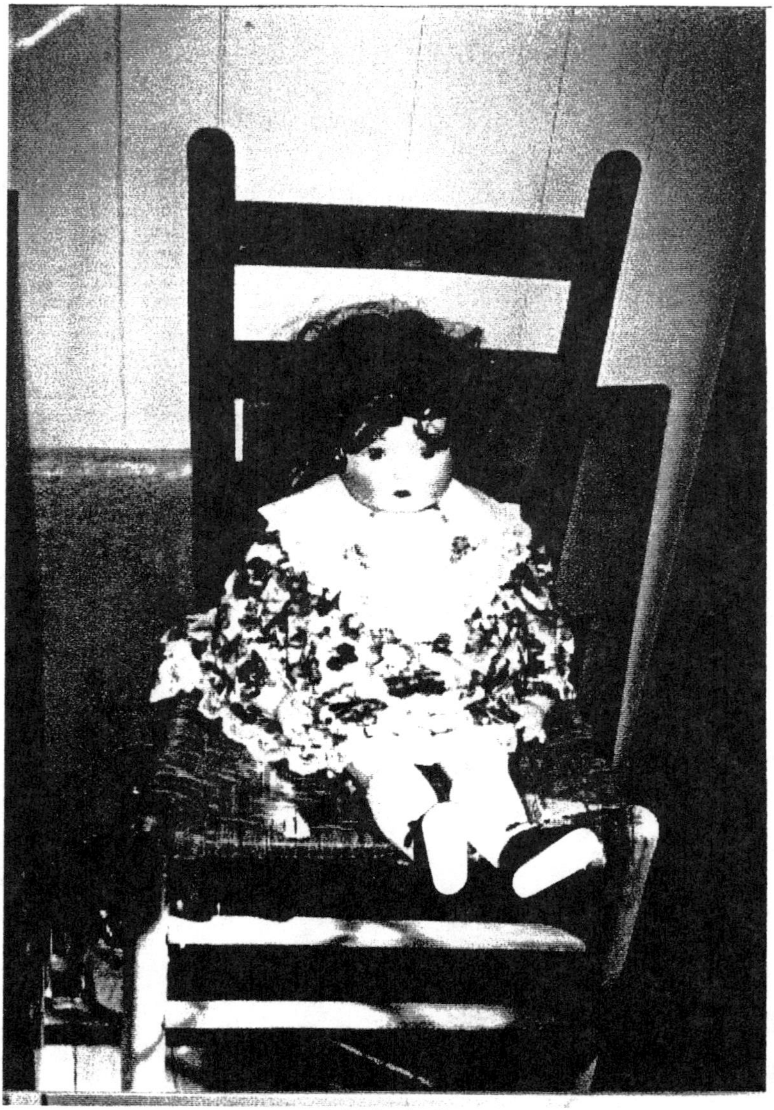

1932 doll

This is the first doll I can remember having. Santa brought it for Christmas. The body is fabric, she is about 24-inches tall. She is sitting in an old homemade chair with split oak bottom.

Hand Made Shoes

In the early years most of the Cataloochee people made their shoes. It took a special talent to make shoes. First they had to cure the leather, soak it in a bath of hickory ashes and water until the hair would come off then they had to scrape off the rest of the hair. The leather would be stiff; they would use mutton or beef tallow to soften the leather.

After all the preparation was finished they had to cut a pattern then cut out the shoe, the sole and the heel. Then it was put on the iron last, the sole and heel was put on with maple pegs, the top was sown with linen thread. The shoes could be repaired when the sole wore thin or the heel run over.

There is a special art to using wooden pegs to construct a shoe, but if you go to Germany today and order a very fine pair of boots I am told that is how they are constructed.

This little child's shoe has been half-soled and the heel appears to have been built up three times. It was plowed up in Big Cataloochee long after they stopped making them.

Sometimes the bears would kill a cow or a calf, they just ate part of it and left the rest of it.

When they found this had happened they would skin out the hide and bring it home and make leather out of it. They used the leather for several purposes; they could make bridles for their horses and some of the harness used on the horses. It's truly amazing how much talent the people had for making most everything they needed in the early years. I suppose they brought some of their knowledge from the old countries coming to America.

Hand-woven Pre Civil War Coverlet.

Used as a bedspread, it was made of wool from the sheep's back and spun into thread which was dyed with indigo, a plant they grew. To weave this intricate design, it is said the woman had to have a keen mind and a sharp memory. There were many beautiful designs and most homes here in the mountains had looms, and most of the women could weave to make coverlets, blankets, cloth for clothes and used wool yarn to knit sweaters, mittens, gloves, sox and toboggans.

Shearing sheep was a very hard job for the men, after shearing they packed the wool in tow sacks. In the early years they had to pick the briars, cocklebures and other trash out of the wool, then the women would wash and dry it before spinning it into thread. After that they would dye it.

Later on the wool was sent to a plant where it was washed, dyed and woven into blankets or cloth.

The first coat that I had, I can remember, was baby blue. The wool had been processed, several blankets were made from it and mother had requested several yards of cloth. She was really a good seamstress; she made my sister and me both blue coats. She made all our clothes until we went to high school.

Spinning Wheels, reels and other things.
Date 1938, photographer: H.C. Wilburn. Photo Courtesy of GSMNP

Where are these flax wheels and spinning wheels: Which were collected for museums in Smoky Mountains Nations Park. They are probably stored in some government storage place. These are from Tennessee same as they used in Cataloochee and other places. See *"Reflections of Cataloochee"* page 210.

Home Made Cradle

A woman could sit and knit, sew, peel apples, break beans or other jobs, while she put her foot on the rocker and rocked the baby to sleep. Getting two jobs done at once. Many did. Almost every family had a cradle.

We feel that the museum pieces should be put in a museum for people to see. Everyone should make a request for these things to be put on display in Cataloochee.

Chapter 9

Cataloochee People Before and After the Park

You may have been misinformed about us mountain people, because for many years outside writers came here, when they found some poor unfortunate family they wrote, implying that we are all ignorant, backward and uncouth. They were only interested in writing something to sell, with total disregard to the truth; therefore, many people have a misconception of us even today.

It is true we were practically isolated in Cataloochee for about one hundred years and many spoke lots of Elizabethan words most were cattlemen and farmers a few were loggers.

We had the small plain little one or two room schools; the teachers were dedicated to their work. When the children finished 7th grade they were sent out to finish their education. Some became successful businessmen some became professionals.

Then there were those who preferred the peace and tranquility of their ancestral home place, they had so much passed down to them, they were happy with farming and raising cattle and other livestock, until the

Park took over. Some of the descendants are still in the cattle business and farming today.

Mrs. Judy Alexander who was raised in Asheville, she and her husband Tom came to Big Cataloochee they had a ranch there for five years, they became friends of the Cataloochee people. Miss Judy remarked in *Mountain Fever*, that the Cataloochee people were high-class mountain people, although she had some trouble understanding their language.

Well its no wonder, the people there had practically been isolated for 100 years and retained much of their Elizabethan speech, some had an Irish brogue and who knows what else.

Mr. Tom Alexander had seen the sad exodus when the people had to move away. He said they were fine old mountain families.

Mr. Ed Trout, Historian for the Great Smoky Mountain National Park played a large part in getting the buildings restored in Cataloochee, he met lots of the natives on many occasions over several years, he got to know them very well. He remarked that he had found the Cataloochee people were of the upper echelon.

There were plenty of outstanding people in Cataloochee, William Mitchel Sutton (see headstone) married Sarah Jane Calwell, daughter of Uncle Harrison Caldwell (there were two other Mitch Suttons later) This Mitch was a mason, his wife was an Eastern Star member. They traveled by buggy to Waynesville, for all the meetings if possible. There were several others in Cataloochee that were members of this organization; according to Mark Hannah, he couldn't recall the names. Gudger Palmer said, "Mitch was really a smart man, he was an esquire (same as lawyer). He helped people who needed advice, wrote up mortgages and deeds and other legal matters, he did all this at little or no cost. Gudger said, "Mitch was very intelligent, he could have been a judge." He and his family lived at the Kerr place, (pronounced Carr Place)

George Palmer and his wife belonged to the Masonic Lodge and she was a member of the Eastern Star. We don't know how many others belonged.

I will list some of the Cataloochee people and what they did after they left Cataloochee and some before.

Robert H Woody: Born 1903 on Little Cataloochee. He became a History Professor and taught at Duke, until he retired. Then he moved to California and lived there the rest of his life, but he never forgot Cataloochee and his people, he returned for as many reunions as possible (read his homecoming speech in this book he really explained how it was living there).

Glenn Palmer: Born in Big Cataloochee after he married they moved to Crabtree where he had a large farm and he served in the State legislature for 20 years. He also served on the Haywood Co. School Board and several other offices in the county. In his young years he was a deputy sheriff with his father William A. Palmer of Big Cataloochee who was the High Sheriff of Haywood County for three terms.

Mark Hannah: born in Little Cataloochee married and had a family, when the Park took over he became the

Park Ranger. He and his family moved to Big Cataloochee where he was the Park Ranger for 31 years.

Gudger Palmer: Born in Big Cataloochee went to college at Chapel Hill, he graduated with a degree in accounting. He worked at Champion Paper in Canton, N.C. until he retired.

Harold Hannah: Born in Little Cataloochee. He worked with Forest Service in Virginia until he retired, he always returned for both Big and Little Cataloochee reunions. He is Master of Ceremonies for the Little Cataloochee reunion.

Joe Palmer: son of Glenn was a State Representative, and then he became a State Senator for many years. He was on the review board for the State prison System, he also served on the State Highway Commission, and he had a large farm in Crabtree and raised cattle.

Eldridge Caldwell: Born in Big Cataloochee moved to Campbell Creek in Maggie Valley where he had a large farm. He became a North Carolina Forest Ranger and worked until he retired, he continued raising beef cattle and had a tenant farmer to take care of his crops and farm. He was elected chairman of the ASC (Agricultural Stabilization and Conservation) in Haywood County 10-1-1965, after his retirement from Forest Service.

William J. Hannah: Born in Little Cataloochee, educated in public school in Waynesville, then went to Wake Forest and the State University from which he graduated with a degree in law. He practiced many years in Waynesville. He was a State Senator in 1912. His son William Tucker Hannah, also to Wake Forest and was a prominent attorney in Waynesville also his son became an attorney. (*Annals of Haywood Co.* Mr. W.C.Allen).

Raymond Caldwell: Born on Big Cataloochee, moved with his parents Bonnie and Jarvis to the Iron Duff Community, they had a large dairy farm. Later Raymond moved to Waynesville, where he had a very successful plumbing business for many years. He bought an airplane and flew for many years.

J.R. Caldwell: Born in Big Cataloochee, had a car and a motor home business in Waynesville many years, until he retired.

Hershal Caldwell: Born in Big Cataloochee brother to Raymond and J.R. He was a barber in Waynesville; he had his own shop there until he retired. He was a barber for fifty-years and twenty-nine days. During WWII he served on the USS New Jersey. He cut the hair of five star Admiral Halsey, 5 star Admiral Nemitz and others. He is now on the North Carolina State Board of Barbers for the past five years. He is a volunteer who has helped maintained trails in Cataloochee for many years.

Helen Hannah (Trantham): Born in Little Cataloochee, went to school there then to Waynesville High School about the time she graduated WWII had started. She went to Washington D.C. worked with the FBI for several years.

Judson Palmer: Was in the military during WWII after it was over he worked at the Pentagon to complete his military retirement, his wife former Hilda Dotson also worked there for the FBI. They retired in Ratcliff Cove.

Horace Woody: Born in Big Cataloochee. He became an executive with the Woolworth Co. After he retired he became president of a Savings and Loan Co. Later he sold real estate in Florida, he was also Mayor of Howey in the Hills, Fl.

Brown Caldwell: Was born in Caldwell Fork, he became a very popular evangelist and was heard on a radio station from Greenville, S.C. for many years.

Riley Palmer: Born in Big Cataloochee graduated from N.C. State. He was the Buncombe County Farm Agent until he retired. He had a large farm in Rush Fork, which he rented out.

Hub Caldwell: Born in Big Cataloochee where he farmed, raised cattle and carried the mail for many years. He moved to Jonathan Creek where he had a large dairy farm until he retired.

Horace Woody son of Steve Woody

Horace Woody was a resident of the Haywood Rest Home in Waynesville N.C. and celebrated his 95th birthday. The alert senior citizen pointed out that it apparently doesn't feel any different to reach one's 95th year.

Woody was perplexed that the rest home employees were making such a fuss over his birthday, noting that "I've already had enough of them."

The former Woolworth's Department Store executive is a native of Haywood County and in fact was "born and raised on Cataloochee and that's as native as they get."

Woody said he was brought up with seven other brothers and sisters in the wilds of Cataloochee" by his parents, Steve and Mary Palmer Woody. His brothers Jonathan and Floyd still reside in Haywood County.

Woody worked with Woolworth's for 35 years as a district manager, residing in 9 southern states and 2 provinces of Canada during his career, and he is, perhaps, one of the few living Americans who can remember the times when department store prices fit the budgets of many.

"We sold nothing for over 10 cents east of the Mississippi," Woody said, "and nothing over 20 cents west of the river." He said that one of the 10-cent items east of the Mississippi was men and women's hose.

These hose, however, cost 10 cents each or 20 cents for a pair, and Woody said he never recalled anyone ever buying half a pair. He added that he had no idea why the hose were sold in this manner.

Some even better bargains were found among the inexpensive items though like a dozen screws for five cents and stove bolts for a penny each.

"The quality of merchandise was better then," Woody said. "People took pride in what they made. Now it's how much they can make.

We had more competition and we had to protect our profits," Woody continued, "so our prices had to go up."

He noted that at one time his stores sold "a good little radio" for $1.99. He said that it was much better than some on the market today.

Woody attended Cataloochee School and then taught there for two years before going on to what was then Clyde Institute for his high-school studies. He also attended several colleges and universities.

He retired from Woolworth's in 1945 and later became president of a building and loan company in Kentucky. Then he went into real estate and later moved to Florida to relax for 20 years. He built a home there as well as another at Lake Junaluska. (*The Mountaineer* June 2, 1976.

L to R: Jonathan H Woody, Joseph H. Way, James T. Noland and Joe S. Davis. Woody became the president of the First National Bank in Waynesville in 1939.

Banker Would Loan to Anyone -- Once
Woody helped build today's First Union

When Jonathan Woody became president of First National Bank in 1939 he sent the community a message:

"He said he'd loan anybody a hundred dollars just to find out whether they would pay him or not," said Linton Palmer a first cousin and former employee of Woody's. "That made people believers. He didn't lose but very little, but it was the best advertising he could have done.

"And if you paid that $100 back and came back the next year to get your crop money, you could get $200, no questions asked."

It wasn't the first time Woody had gotten Haywood County's attention. People had doubted he could buy controlling interest in the bank, a move, he accomplished in late 1939, at age 43.

Jonathan's children, Steve Woody and Laura Woody Soltis, tell how their father went back to his home in Cataloochee to let them know he'd purchased controlling shares of J.R. Boyd's Bank. Jonathan's father was Steve Woody, also known as "Uncle Steve."

"Uncle Steve liked a little drink, so Woody carried him a pint," wrote Soltis. "They were sitting around with some neighbors having a drink, and Uncle Steve said, 'What's the news from Waynesville?' Jonathan said, 'Well, today I bought Jim Boyd's bank.' They all looked at each other and Uncle Steve said, 'pour us another drink and tell us another big lie.'"

Woody had grown up in Cataloochee, gone to school at Western Carolina (then Cullowhee Normal Industrial School) and the University of South Carolina, where he sold apples from back home to meet expenses. He had worked at the Bank of Waynesville for about three years, and then worked as a credit manager in Atlanta. He then worked for a printing company before becoming a bank examiner with the Federal Deposit Insurance Corp. Now he was coming home.

The purchase also caught bank owner J.R. Boyd a little by surprise, according to Linton Palmer. Boyd had put out word the bank was for sale, and several people had made deposits but been unable to come up with the full purchase price. Woody visited from Atlanta and paid Boyd a $500 deposit. According to Palmer, Boyd went next door to bank vice president Reeves Noland and told him, "We've just made ourselves another $500. That young whippersnapper thinks he can buy our bank."

But Jonathan Woody could raise the money. As a bank examiner, Woody had traveled in Georgia, Florida,

Alabama, Mississippi and Atlanta. According to Soltis and Steve Woody, their father was asked by a Florida executive to make recommendations for his banks. Impressed with his work, the executive asked if Woody would like to be a vice president at one of his banks, or would he like to manage a bank in Florida? Woody said he wanted to own a bank in Western North Carolina.

When Woody was ready, the executive told him, the Florida bank would loan him the money, at low interest. So a couple of days after he made the deposit, Woody returned to Boyd with the full purchase price.

Woody became president of First National Bank of Waynesville on Jan. 10, 1940, and started using the slogan "The Friendly Bank." His emphasis was on people, according to Palmer and his children. He loaned people money on their word. He took pride in loaning money to mountain youth for college and claimed he never lost money on that kind of loan.

Customers returned that trust.

"He would be walking down the street, and somebody would pull a roll of bills out of their overalls. I guess maybe after the tobacco money came in, and give it to him to pay on their loan," said Soltis. "And he'd make a note of it and take it back to the bank. Can you imagine bank people doing that today?"

Bank promotion

Woody held a strong interest in farming. It led to one of his most spectacular marketing ploys. In the autumn of 1945, Woody bought Haywood County's grand champion steer from young Ted Francis. The steer became the guest of the bank for a day, set up with his own fence, hay, feed and water bucket, as well as the young Francis to keep him company. Woody hoped the move would not only promote his bank but also encourage farmers to improve the breeding in their cattle, said his son.

Woody encouraged residents to make improvements on their farms and homes. He teamed up with then extension director Wayne Corpening to promote community development clubs and encouraged their involvement in countywide issues.

"People came to the bank to borrow money to build a home," wrote Soltis in a list of her father's accomplishments. "If they promised to put in inside plumbing, they got the loan."

Woody also promoted industry, helping negotiate the purchase of land for what became the Dayco plant and providing a site for the beginnings of Wellco. He worked with tourism developers, including Carl Henry, the recently deceased founder of Twinbrook in Maggie Valley.

"If you would work and do what you told him you were going to do, you got the money," Henry said of Woody in a 1997 interview. Woody's support "beat anything you ever saw," he said.

The banker was also active in First Methodist Church of Waynesville, serving as chairman of stewards. He chaired the board of directors at Western Carolina University for about eight years was a trustee of Bevard

College and chairman of the library board, among other activities. He also loved golfing and fishing, said Soltis, and made frequent visits back to Cataloochee. He emceed the Cataloochee Reunion for many years, a task his son, Steve, now assumes.

Business Mentor

With all his activities, Jonathan Woody remained focused on banking. About 1946 he organized the First State Bank of Hazelwood and became its president. Later he purchased the Transylvania Trust Company of Bevard and became its president.

Meanwhile, his cousin, Linton Palmer, had graduated from college. Jonathan Woody, who was more like a father figure than a cousin, encouraged Palmer to try banking and after repeated offers, Palmer accepted. Palmer would remain with First National throughout its mergers into First Union for his entire 36-year career.

Woody encouraged Palmer to take a leadership role, Palmer remembered, sending him to many training sessions. As a manager, the bank president was very hands-on he said.

"He wanted to know everything that went on and have a part to play in all decisions made at the bank," Palmer said.

"He was a very good employer," Palmer Added. "He looked after his employees better than anyone I ever knew or worked for. If you had a problem at home, he was involved in it and looked after you."

Woody was president of North Carolina Bankers Association in 1952, where he worked to obtain retirement plans for bank employees.

Though he was president of three banks, Woody dreamed of a regional bank, Palmer said. So about a year after Palmer began working at First National, it merged with First National Bank of Asheville, which was controlled by Charlie Parker. The Bevard Bank was also part of the merger. The Bank of Asheville had a branch in Hendersonville, so the resulting merger created a bank with branches in four counties. The next year the

Haywood County Bank, based in Canton, became part of the regional bank.

But in the next couple of years, "Charlie Parker and Mr. Woody didn't see everything eye to eye," Palmer said. Woody, who with his stockholder friends retained control of the Haywood and Transylvania branches, disagreed with some of Parker's decisions. And Woody had a solution.

"He and his associates heard that Union Bank of Charlotte was wanting to be a regional bank," Palmer said. So Woody contacted the president and chairman of the board of Union National Bank of Charlotte. The result was a merger on July 18, 1958, that created First Union National Bank.

Banking Merger

Jonathan Woody retired from the bank he helped create a couple of years later, Palmer said. At first, it was a rough transition for a man used to being a part of every decision.

Then a bank in Sarasota, Fla., contacted Woody. It was having problems, its officers said, and needed someone to straighten it out and train a new leader. Woody spent more than a year in Florida with that bank before returning to Haywood County.

Today, First Union, the bank Woody helped to create, is the sixth-largest bank in the nation and is asking stockholders to consider a merger with Wachovia.

If that merger were approved, the resulting bank would have 19 million customers.

Woody lived to see First Union expand statewide and throughout the South. He died in 1981, at the age of 85.

"He never forgot where he came from," Linton Palmer said.

And, his children added, he often said that he was "doing pretty well for a Cataloochee boy."[1]

---

[1] This article first appeared in *The Enterprise Mountaineer*. Written by Kathy N. Ross who gave me permission to use it.

Hubert Caldwell son of Hub & Maude Caldwell
Photo: courtesy of Gilmer Caldwell

Hubert Caldwell: son of Hub born in Big Cataloochee, grew up in Jonathan Creek Community went to Waynesville High School then WWII happened. He got in the Air Force, he loved flying after the war he worked with Pan AM over thirty years.

Ken J. Caldwell: Son Of Eldridge born in Big Cataloochee went to Waynesville High School, then to the University of NC at Cullowhee. He taught school in Virginia, and then he went to work with the Veterans Hospital and worked there until he retired. His hobby was flying also both of his sons Phil and Jack and his nephew Gil Grasty and his 1st cousin Kyle Campbell all pilots of pleasure, except Ken's youngest son Ken Jackson Jr. who is a helicopter pilot with Las Vegas Police Force.

Tommy Caldwell: Born on Big Cataloochee, moved to Utah Mountain with his wife and 14 children. They owned and operated a very large dairy and bought more land. Some of the family lives on the same place.

Floyd Woody: Had farmed in Big Cataloochee, he moved to Canton and bought an interest in Smather's Oil Co. He and his wife Falsom, continued to live there the rest of their life. Floyd was very quick witted, a jolly fellow with lots of jokes and fun for all.

Jarvis Palmer: Born on Big Cataloochee farmed, raised cattle and other livestock. He had several cottages in which he rented to fishermen and others. He owned a lot of land along the creek; he and his brother Harley let people fish for 50¢ per day. When he moved out of Cataloochee he bought a nice big farm in Jonathan Creek where he raised fine beef cattle.

Linton Palmer: son of Jarvis born on Big Cataloochee he was only five years old when they had to move away. He could remember his Aunt Mirair crying all the way across the mountain when they were evicted. (See *Reflections of Cataloochee)* He graduated from NC State. He became a banker and was a banker at First Union National Bank in Waynesville, N.C. for 31 years.

Clay McGaha a Cataloochee man remembered going to the First Union National Bank to borrow $400.00, his wife had to have surgery but the hospital in Franklin said they would not operate until he paid the $400.00. He came back to Waynesville to the First Union National Bank and tried to borrow the money but was turned down, this was when Jonathan Woody first started at the bank, and someone else had turned Clay down. He was upset, just didn't know what to do he started out of the bank, Jonathan saw him, and asked him to come into his office. Clay told his story, Jonathan said Clay, sign here. Clay never forgot that. It is just one of the many, many stories of his helping people. He said he never lost a penny on loans.

Steve Woody: Son of Jonathan went to UNC at Chapel Hill in which he earned his BS and MBA degrees. He worked at First Union National Bank in Waynesville, N.C. He was a Naval Officer for 3 ½ years. Today (2002) he is Chief Operating Office and Executive Vice President of Mills Mfg. Co. in Weaverville, N.C. He was on the board of trustees of UNC at Cullowhee for 16 years. Steve was one of the founders of Friends of the Smokies. He is our Master of Ceremonies at the Big Cataloochee Reunion, which we appreciate, his father Jonathan was in charge of it until he passed away.

Mr. Will Messer: Born on Big Cataloochee later settled on Little Cataloochee. It was said he was Jack-of-all-trades who could make anything he wanted of iron or wood. His niece Beatrice Sisk said, he was a "well read, very intelligent, money-making man, and everything he touched turned to money." He worked continuously to improve his farm and equipment. He invented a machine to speed up the process of making shingles for the roof. He bought a steam engine to run his sawmill and a gasoline engine to turn his gristmill. He owned the first touring car and pickup truck in Little Cataloochee.

His big house was the largest and finest structure in Little Cataloochee. It had eleven rooms, hot and cold water and was lit by an acetylene system.

Mail Carrier

There were several mail carriers over the years when Cataloochee was a thriving community. I have written about others in *"Reflections of Cataloochee Valley."*

Today December 26, 2001 I interviewed Vaughn Palmer, he is now 99 years of age, with a very clear mind, carried the mail eight years by horse and buggy along with his brother Vernon who carried it part of the time. This meant getting up at 4 o'clock and feed his horse, then eat breakfast, and then start out.

Vaughn went to the post office and picked up the mail which was in leather bags with locks on them, when he arrived at Cove Creek post office the bags would be unlocked, the mail taken out and mail that had arrived from Waynesville would be transferred to the bags, locked back and given to Vaughn to carry back to Cataloochee.

He said, "I always carried my lunch, I had a lunch pail, my mother would fix it up with ham and biscuits and what ever she had maybe beans other food. That was a twenty-four mile round trip."

When asked about snow, he said, "yes lawsey me yes, plenty of it, sometimes knee deep or more. In the wintertime it would turn dark on me at Bennett turn. (The first sharp curve opposite Boyd Mountain). At Christmas time the buggy would have such a heavy load and the road so bad, lots of time the mud was so deep I could hear the horse pull his feet out with every step. I would get out of the buggy and walk. I had the horse trained to pull the buggy and I would walk behind.

"Other times when it was so awful cold I had a blanket to cover me, I kept a lantern under the blanket for a little warmth, but I got my ears frostbitten.

"Lots of time there was so much ice, oh just ice everywhere. I had my horse tipped."

I inquired and found that he had the horseshoes turned down on the ends so the tips could cut into the ice like cleats. He said that's the only way he got up the icy mountain. He said Jarvis Palmer was a good blacksmith. He would tip my horseshoes for me.

Vaughn said one time when his brother Vernon was carrying the mail, he stopped to pick huckleberries, the horse looked around and saw his chance to run away, so he ran away and tore up the buggy.

Vaughn said I have hauled lots of snuff and tobacco to some of them folks in Cataloochee before William and Milia built the store there was no snuff and tobacco in Cataloochee.

They let me build a garage near the store when I returned from my mail run; I unhooked the buggy and left it there, then rode my horse on home.

Vaughn said at a later time his brother Kimsey had a car and carried the mail up over Mt. Sterling on down to Newport, Tennessee.

In 1925 Vaughn bought a Ford truck, in 1928 he married Magola Caldwell (my great Uncle Andy's daughter). They moved out of Cataloochee to Dellwood and lived with her sister, Faye Davis, and then they lived with Charlie Palmer near Waynesville. Vaughn worked at the Tannery in Hazelwood for eighteen months, his wages were $14.10 per week, and then he built a service station and house near Dellwood, and then built a station and house near Mooney Cove Road, his wife and family helped at the station. Vaughn drove a station wagon to take work hands to work at Enka. Then he bought a bus and hauled more people to work. Not many people had a car in those days, 1920's and 1930's. He provided a service people needed in order to have a job. He drove all three shifts, later he bought two buses and drove for forty years to both Champion at Canton and to the Enka Rayon Plant.

Robert Vance Hannah Sr. born in Little Cataloochee 1884-1898? He went to school there, we are not sure where he went to high school, late around 1817 he went to Berea College Ky. for one year, he majored in accounting. He worked for the War Department several years, he was drafted in 1918 and he was sent overseas. He met and married Hazel LeMarquais 1921 they became active in the Baptist Church in Arlington, Va. where they lived for 18 years. They had a 240-acre farm.

He worked for several private firms in the 30s. Then in the 40s he joined the Rural Electric Administration, he retired in 1963-64 as GS 15. He had traveled all over U.S. to establish REA Coop. And he helped Western Carolina to get electricity.

Maggie Brown Kauffman R.N.
Photo courtesy: Dora Brown Warren

Maggie Brown Kauffman born on Little Cataloochee daughter of Jonah and Sychia Coggins Brown. She went to school in Little Cataloochee then to Aston Park in Asheville, N.C. where she trained to be a nurse. World War II came along and since she was a nurse and joined the Air Force she could enter in as a Lutientent and served in Germany and Japan and other places during the war, afterwards she stayed in service until she retired in Colorado Springs, Colorado with rank of Captain. After she retired she lived in Asheville with her husband and family.

There were most surely many others who were born and raised in Cataloochee that went out into the world and were successful, but at this time, this is all the information that I have.

We have been out of that beautiful valley about seventy years now, I am certain this is only a portion of the information, but it's enough to wipe out that stereotype that the mountain people were portrayed to be, by those fiction writers of years ago.

Some Descendants of Young Bennett

About 1840 Young Bennett sold his 50 acres of land at East Fork and moved into the Cataloochee wilderness with his wife and four young sons. Their cabin was separated from that of the Levi Caldwell family by a dogtrot, and the two families were among the first to settle that area. According to Elizabeth Powers, in her book *Cataloochee, the Lost Settlement in the Smokies,* the Cataloochee community turned to Young "Dock" Bennett when they were sick, continuing nearly two decades after the end of the Civil War.

The Bennett family history, written by Mrs. Herma Messer, who knew Young Bennett personally and was his great granddaughter, states:

> Young Bennett's education was mostly self-acquired. He was a great student of the Bible and such other books as he could get, especially medical books. In his day it was a difficult job to get a doctor into the Cataloochee Valley, so they all came to him for help. He refused to be a midwife except in emergencies, but he treated their diseases and set their broken bones, sometimes staying in their homes for days to care for the seriously ill. He would send to Waynesville for a supply of staple drugs and keep them on hand. But he also used many of the native herbs, roots, and barks in his practice.

Recent research reveals that Young Bennett's father, Hardiman Bennett, was also a doctor, practicing in Haywood County in the 1830's and 1840's at the East Fork of the Pigeon River. Receipts at the Wilson Library of the University of North Carolina show payments to Dr. Hardiman Bennett for treatment of members of the Thomas Lenoir family.

Young Bennett married Elvira "Allie" Mease in 1832. She was the sister of Peter Mease, who was the father of Dr. J.M. Mease. This union began a long line of physisicans and medical professionals, as documented in *Heritage of Healing: A Medical History of Haywood County*, by Nina L. Anderson and William L. Anderson. At least six of Young and Elvira's grandsons became physicians.

One of their songs Archibald Lafayette Bennett, died during the Civil War from injuries he received at Murfreesboro (Stone River), leaving behind a widow and two young children. The son, Aurelius McDonald Bennett, was one year old when his father was killed. He became a doctor, graduating from the Louisville (Kentucky) Medical College in 1885, having first "read" medicine with Dr. Charles Roberts in Crabtree. After a brief practice in Jackson County, he moved to Bryson City, where at one time he served as mayor, and established his medical practice there in the Bennett Building. His son Dr. Percival Bennett entered the practice with him after graduating from the University of Maryland at Baltimore in 1916. Dr. Percival Bennett's brother was Dr. Kelly Bennett a pharmacist at Bryson City.

Dr. Miles Bennett, son of Jasper Newton Bennett and Jalie Gillett Bennett, was the second of Young Bennett's grandsons to become a physician. He was a graduate of Vanderbilt Medical College and practiced several years in Texas before moving to Colombia, South America, to serve as the doctor for a railroad company.

His brother was Dr. David Bennett (the fourth of Young Bennett's grandsons to become a physician). He also graduated from Vanderbilt Medical College and practiced in Oklahoma until his death.

The fifth and six grandsons of Young Bennett who became physicians were from his daughter, Sophronia. She married Marion Rice after the Civil War, and they moved to Georgia. Two of their sons, whose names I do not know, became physicians at Marietta, Georgia.

Two grandsons of Creighton Bennett and Matilda Caldwell Bennett became dentists. They were Dr. Charles Bennett and Dr. Gola Bennett.

In addition to these in the medical profession, it is noteworthy that one of Young Bennett's grandsons, Oscar Bennett (son of Newton and Jalie Bennett), graduated from the University of North Carolina and was a respected attorney in Asheville for many years. His son, Harold also graduated from the University of North Carolina and was at one time president of the North Carolina bar, among numerous other honors.

Another grandson, Thorton Randolph Bennett, was also an attorney, and his brother George was a professor.

Two of Young Bennett's grandsons were ministers. John Carmine Bennett, my grandfather, was a Baptist minister; known primarily for his service at the Hominy Baptist Church at Candler, which he helped to rebuild after a devastating fire, and the Enka Baptist Church, which he founded. His brother was Dr. Hardy Bennett, a Methodist minister in New York City.

One of Young Bennett's great grandsons was Dr. Willis Bennett, who was dean of theology, the Provost, at the Southern Baptist Seminary in Louisville. Another Dr. Harold Bennett was a prominent Baptist minister who was active worldwide with the Southern Baptist Convention, some years ago.

There are others whose names and information I do not have immediately available. Among them there are numerous teachers, university professors and administrators, dairy farmers, nurses and other medical professionals, and business owners and leaders. All of them that I have personally met have a keen sense of family history and the values that forebears such as Young and Allie Bennett passed down through more than a century: Hard work, perseverance, duty to others, and the need to make a difference.[1]

---

[1] This information from Carolyn Bennett Mahaffey, Atlanta Georgia

Chapter 10

Stitching Mama's Fingers Back on and other Tales of Grandma.

(A descendant of William Reddy Noland of Cataloochee as told by her daughter, Louise Brooks Snyder)

Times were hard in the late 30's and early 40's for these were part of the Great Depression. For my three brothers, and me they were happy years. We had to come to live with our Conner grandparents (our dad had been killed by a train four years earlier and Mama Carrie had remarried.) We would not realize until many years after what a load they took on. They loved us and taught us truth and honesty.

Although they had raised nine children of their own, they opened their hearts and their home to us. To this day I don't know how they did it.

Grandpa Lee Conner was a big, strong man of Irish descent. His family had come from Lincoln County, N.C. to the Webster Township in the 1850's. He and his three brothers had worked on the railroad from Asheville to Murphy. He didn't talk much but what he said was the truth. His favorite saying was "If there's anything people hate it's a rogue and a liar" I did not ever want to be a rogue or a liar.

Granny Mary was a tiny woman with snow-white hair. She wore it in a neat ball on the back of her head. She lived by the golden rule, always ready to lend a helping hand to anyone in need. She could feed table after table on Sunday. The women would wash dishes and reset the table. Her father, Nicholas Hoyle was German and her mother was Martha "Matt" Noland who was of Irish ancestry and is the grandma Matt later on in this story.

Our house was made of big round logs and had been built by Grandpa and his sons. It had two big rooms in front with a porch that went from one end of the house to the other and of course, there was a fireplace. The kitchen and its porch were off to the back. Under this house was a cellar with shelves all around filled with jars of pickled beans, pickled beets, kraut and fruits. In the center was a spring. Outside she grew flowers of every kind and color.

A picket fence, to keep the animals out, enclosed the garden. We had a cow named "Red" and a mule named "Trim" and Grandpa's faithful old dog "Rock". There were children everywhere.

We knew all the cousins and loved them dearly. They all have great memories of those days also.

In the evenings when work was done, we'd gather sometimes at my Uncle George's house for music. He was a well-known fiddler. Young musicians would bring their guitars and banjos and their mandolins to play along with George.

Other times we'd all gather around Granny's and Grandpa's rocking chairs on the front porch to listen to stories about the old days stories about the railroad, floods, death and disease about that awful flu that killed so many of their kin eleven in 2 weeks.

Nicholas & Martha "Matt" Noland Hoyle

Granny Mary's father was a German. The Nicholas Hoyle family had lived in Pennsylvania before coming to N.C. Her mother was Martha "Matt" Noland a descendant of William Noland of Cataloochee. Her grandfather was Philip Noland. The Nolands along with the Hannahs were some of the first settlers of Little

Cataloochee and have several landmarks named for them.

I loved those old stories about Grandma Matt riding off on her horse to help some woman in need in childbirth. She wore her hair tied back with a kerchief and her skirts were down to her buttoned shoes.

My favorite one though was about my Mama's fingers when she was 7 years old. It was May 12th 1915. There was much excitement around the Conner household for a new baby was coming any minute!

Grandma Matt was a midwife; she was busy getting things laid out of her little black bag. The water was boiling and her daughter Mary was getting close to delivery.

The children had been sent outside to fine something to do. Carrie (my Mom) and her sister Martha decided to chop wood. Carrie would push the pole forward and Martha would chop. Suddenly off came three fingers! Carrie started running, screaming to the top of her lungs. Martha was right behind her screaming just as loud.

Meantime the chickens had run off with the fingers! Grandpa hollered, Oh Lordy Mercy! Catch them chickens get them fingers before they eat them. The boys ran the chickens down and grabbed those fingers and brought them to Grandma Matt, She washed the dirt off, of course there was nothing to deaden the pain, then she stuck the fingers back on with brown sugar and turpentine and stitched them with white thread. She strapped the hand on a board to heal. Poor little Carrie cried herself to sleep.

Little Henry was born soon after, adding his crying to Carrie's when she woke up. Grandma Matt stayed on for a few days until her daughter Mary, baby Henry and Little Carrie were all on the mend.

Mama Carrie learned to use her sewn on fingers very well she played the banjo and played the organ. She also sang and danced. We loved it when she'd come to pick and sing for us. She played with Uncle George and those young musicians too.

Granny could sang too. She would sing, "I am bound for the Promised land" and "Barbara Allen". It was great to hear the music.

Mama lived to be eighty-six years old and never tired of telling about her fingers. She made quilts, picked her guitar and did anything else she needed to do with her fingers. The white cotton string worked out of her fingers for years, but her fingers healed perfectly except the forefinger was a wee bit crocked.

Carrie Conner Brooks Queen

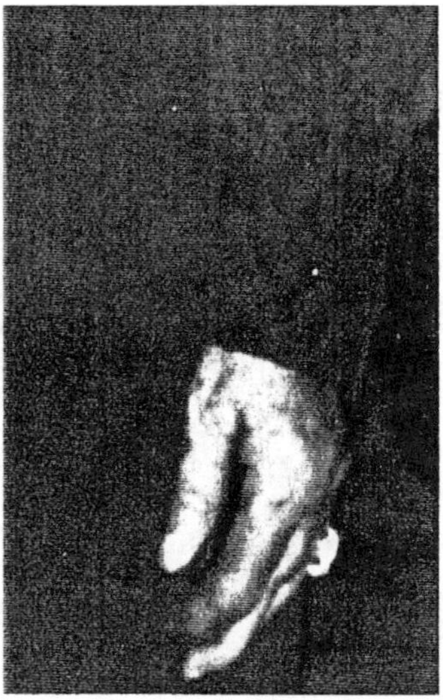

Carrie's fingers
See how it healed.

In her later years she suffered with arthritis and when she was sent to Asheville to a doctor, he was amazed at her hand. After hearing her story he told her that Grandma Matt had made medical history and just didn't know it.

I'm very proud of my heritage and I hope I have a little bit of their character. Those were great people.

By: Louise Brooks Snyder

Waynesville, N.C.

Chapter 11

Nailon

Thomas Naillon

Thomas, a brother to Mary Ann Naillon Caldwell

Affectionately known as "Granny Pop"

Naillon Family
Can you help identify them?
Email: JTWiggie@aol.com

Naillon Town, Tennessee

Naillon Town was a small community located one mile above Hartford, Tennessee. This small community consisted of several families and one small store. Jim Ike and Eva Lee Gates operated the store during the fifties.

The first Post Office in the area was Naillon; it opened October 8, 1880. This Post Office was opened due to Elijah W. Naillon and A. Pollas Bryant. Naillon was a Post Office for 35 years before it was discontinued on April 1, 1916, when rural delivery was established from Hardford.

When construction of I-40 began, the small community of Naillon Town disappeared.

Naillon Post Office

Cocke County, Tennessee

USPS Historian, Corporate Information

Name	Title	Date Appointed
Elijoh V. Naillon	Postmaster	10/08/1880
Isaac Cates	Postmaster	02/09/1883
John Ford	Postmaster	10/04/1883
Reuben P. Clark	Postmaster	07/17/1901
Joseph S. Green	Postmaster	04/15/1902
Lewis S. Rains	Postmaster	03/23/1911
William B. Ford	Postmaster	08/03/1911

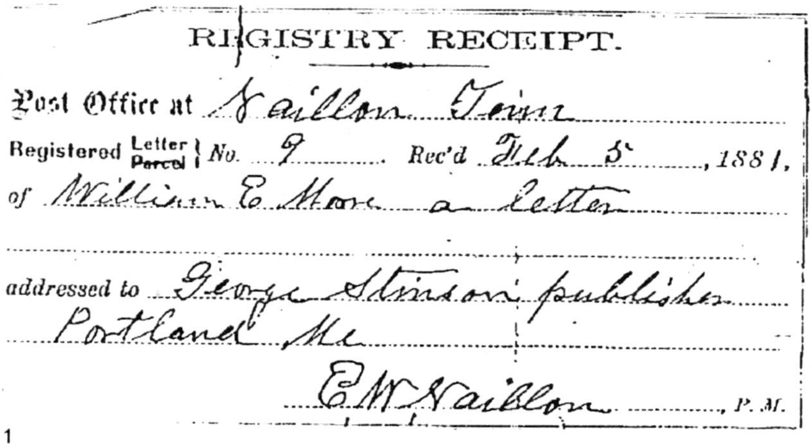

REGISTRY RECEIPT.

Post Office at Naillon Tenn

Registered Letter/Parcel No. 9 Rec'd Feb 5, 1881,

of William E. Moore a letter

addressed to George Stinson publisher Portland Me

E W Naillon, P. M.

1

[1] Junior and Helen Ball, 54 Hale Brook Rd. New Port, TN

Husband: Patrick Naillon

Born: 1769 In: County Cork Ireland

Married: About 1825 In Green Co. TN

Died: 1833 In: Paint Mountain, N.C.

Other Spouses: Unknown

Wife: Frances Russell

Born: About 1795 In Green Co. TN

Died: 1866 In Jefferson Co. TN

Other Spouses: ? Sutherland

Children:

1) Name: Elijah Washington Naillon

Born: 10-26-1826 in Buncombe Co. NC

Died: 7-27-1904

Spouses: Nancy Moore, Harriet Brown, Margaret Gates

Husband: Patrick Naillon

Born: 1769 In: County Cork Ireland

Died: 1833 In: Paint Mountain, N.C.

Other Spouses: Frances Russell

Wife: Unknown

Children:

1) Name: Catherine Naillon

Born about 1807 In NC

Married: About 1824 In: Tenn

Died: About 1877 In Burnet County Tx

2) Name: William Naillon

Born: 1809

3) Name: James Robert Naillon

Born 1812 In NC

Married: 1-30-1838

Died: 12-21-1890

4) Name: John B. Naillon

Born 1815 In NC

Spouse: Mary Polly Dalton

5) Name: Mary Ann Naillon*

Born: 5-27-1817 In Madison County NC

Married: About 1836

Died: 2-18-1891

Spouse: Levi Belese Caldwell

6) Name: Thomas Naillon

Born: 3-18-1818 In Rutherford Co. TN

Married: 1-01-1839 In Rutherford Co. NC

Died: 6-28-1899 In Dalton, Whitfield Co.

GA

Spouse: Elizabeth Harriet Cochran

Prepared by: Jean Turner Wigglesworth

7385 leisure Lane

Mason, Ohio 45040

e-mail: J.T.Wiggie@aol.com

Naillion Swinging bridge across the Pigeon River 1947.

It would be interesting to know how many descendants, but I think it would be quite impossible since the families were so large and spread all over the United States, Maybe some foreign countries and given the long period of time, of course there are more coming along all the time. I am convinced we will never run out of Cataloochee descendants.

Naillon

Mary Ann Naillon, affectionately known as Granny Pop, we did not know much about the Naillons until recently, when we received genealogy from one descendant, Mrs. Jean Wiggleworth, also information from Junior and Helen Ball.

We find the Naillons also to be quite an extended large family.

Chapter 12

Cataloochee Reunion Looms, Bring Back Old Memories

(Nola's Memories)

Once again Sunday, as they have every second Sunday in August for 50-plus years, the remnants and descendents of Cataloochee will return.

They will travel the twisted and narrow gravel road up the mountain from Cove Creek and down the other side of the Great Smoky Mountains National Park, to a high mountain valley their families left more than half a century ago.

They come back to see old friends, to see the newest and newborn descendents of Cataloochee families. They come to share food, and remember those who have died since their last gathering. And those who can cram into Palmer's Chapel will worship again in what was once a Methodist Church for the Big Cataloochee Community. It is also a time for remembering, Nola Conard Jones has a lot of memories from both Little and Big Cataloochee. At 94, she is among the oldest still living that was born in Cataloochee, decades before it became part of the National Park. He brother, Pless Conard, at 88, has his share of memories as well.

Conard families farmed on Little Cataloochee, across the ridge from the larger community that shared its name. The rich soil of "Little Cataloochee" holds still in her mind.

"We could grow everything in Cataloochee you could grow, everything," she said. "It was black dirt." For a child, however, that black dirt could also tell its secrets.

"We had lots of hogs, and we had to go feed them in the woods," Jones said. "It's dark in the woods, and I'm afraid of the woods. So we buried the corn (meant for the hogs) up and down the edge of the woods. We didn't have sense enough to know it could come up."

When the corn sprouted along the woods, Jones' father quickly figured out it had never been fed to the hogs. Nola wouldn't confess, but her brother did. So Nola was disciplined, she remembered, not so much for burying the corn as for refusing to tell the truth.

While the practice of free-range grazing had almost stopped in Big Cataloochee by the time they were children, it was still common on Little Cataloochee, said Nola and her brother, Pless, 89.

The practice was to fence in what needed to be protected, Pless said, including the crops and the apple orchards. Then the hogs and sometimes cattle were marked and allowed to range the woods. In the fall, after the apples were picked, sometimes the hogs or cattle would be turned into the orchard to clean up the dropped fruit.

About every family also had honeybees. Pless said, using honey as a sweetener year round.

Nola, Pless and their younger sister, Odette Johnson, now 77, are the last three of a family that once included five siblings from their father's first marriage and 10 from his second marriage to their mother.

Those large families were common on Cataloochee, Pless said, reciting names of families who had 12 and 11 children.

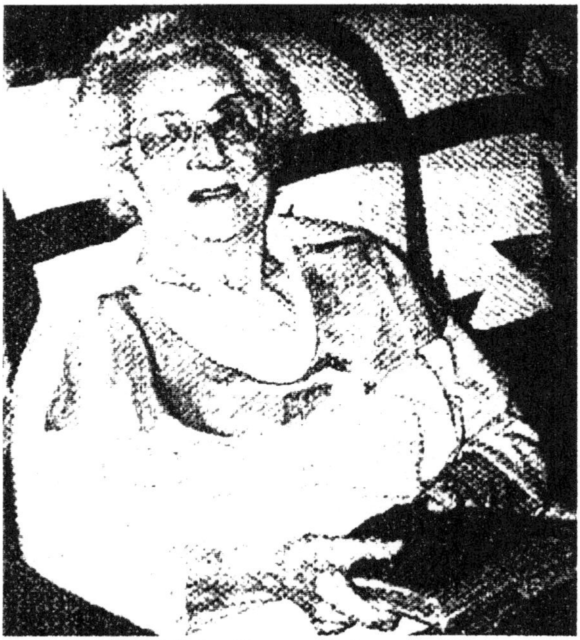

Nola Conard Jones

Nola Conard, born in Little Cataloochee, talked about driving a wagon loaded with apples to Big Creek.

Lord I hated that drive, it was dangerous work, and you really had to hold down on that brake. All the family would go in the woods and gather bushels of chestnuts and haul them to Big Creek, there they could ship apples and chestnuts by train to Knoxville! They could get .50 to .75 per bushel.

When Nola was twelve years old she went to live in Crabtree with Glenn Palmer and his wife to help with their children and dairy. She lived with them more than 10 years. The Palmers went to Asheville to see "Gone with the Wind" They took Nola with them, it was her first movie, then she did not see another movie until she was 40 years old. After they returned to Crabtree, she named all of the dairy cows after characters in the movie.

In 1927 Mrs. Palmer gave Nola a Bible for Christmas she said, Nola always live up to the teaching of this divine book.

After the National Park was created and bought land from the people, promising they could continue to live there the rest of their life, but eventually forced the people out. The Conard family moved to Hartford, Tennessee. Like other families it was a very sad time, they eventually got settled, but it took many years to feel at home in a different place.[1]

---

[1] *Enterprise Mountaineer* By Kathy N. Ross

Chapter 13

History in the Making

Cataloochee Valley, N.C. in the Great Smoky Mountain National Park, a cold frosty morning in February 2000 the huge tents were erected, a large crowd of people, about a thousand gathered there. There was great excitement, the elk are coming! The elk are coming back!

Photo Courtesy of Hershel Caldwell

History was made when the Park Service and other wildlife-concerned groups were able to transport 25 elk into Cataloochee Valley as an experimental elk restoration program. The Park Service says the elk roamed freely here 200 years ago.

The elk were brought from land between the Lakes National Recreation area, which is near the Tennessee-Kentucky border. A big rig arrived with the elk. The elk were put in a three acre holding pen in Cataloochee for a couple of months, until they were accustomed to their new surroundings. The pen was up a steep hill with an old narrow road.

A large tractor pulled the trailer load of elk, through the creek and up the hill to the pen.

Photo Courtesy of Hershel Caldwell

In order to keep from frightening the elk the Park Service had erected a wooden wall with small round holes for people to look through and see the elk.

There was a lady veterinarian who came to check on the elk, she had a large motor home and lab. combined.

When the gate to the pen was opened, some of the elk went out to explore their new territory, while others stayed in the pen several days before going out in the new territory.

Photo Courtesy of Hershel Caldwell

Eight of the elk were expected to have calves. A transmitter had been implanted in the birth canal so with the birth of a calf it would drop and start sending signals. The researchers could know when and where one was born.

They could find the transmitter long before they could find the calf, because the mother would hide the calf away from the birth site. The mother knows the first few days the elk calves are most vulnerable to predators. They can walk in a few minutes after they are born, in about three days; they are able to follow their mother.

When elk calves are born they have camouflaged spotted coats like the white tailed deer fawns that is nature's way to help hide the baby from predator and the reason they are so hard to find.

While the herd is out grazing one or more females take turns baby-sitting.

History was made again on Friday June 22, 2001 when the first male elk was born in Cataloochee in possibly 200 year; he weighed 40 pounds.

The baby elk depend on mothers' milk for about a month then they start to graze, but will continue to suckle until they are about nine months old. After that they graze on the lush tender grass of Cataloochee.[1]

"One of the long term goals is to have a huntable population" Rick Varner, a Park Resource Manager said. To manage any kind of large game animals, you need money - and big game hunting is a main source of contributions.

"Once elk wander out side the Park jurisdiction they could be hunted," Varner said. The Kentucky-Tennessee border was the site of an elk release five years ago. This year (2002) the recreation area has already started an elk-hunting season, said Barry Holbert, co-chairman of the Western North Carolina Chapter of the Rocky Mountain Elk Foundation.

---

[1] *National Park News*

All species inside the Park are protected from hunting or poaching if elk wander into nearby property that is designated a "No Elk Zone," however, landowners would have the right to shoot them.

Varner requested that no one shoots the elk until an elk season is enacted and the population is allowed to grow. Radio collars will constantly track the elk. When they are in "NO Elk Zone" the rangers will catch the animal and return it to the Park.

We are asking people just to give us a call and give us a chance, Varner said; we will capture it and remove it.[1]

Poaching an elk inside the Park would fall under federal wildlife laws, which carry very steep fines

Most elk shed their antlers in the springtime, usually in March, and then they immediately begin growing new ones. The antlers are very rich in calcium; rodents and other animals eat them right away.

In late spring elk shed their winter coat and start growing a new sleek copper colored one, a thin summer coat.

Most calves are born in early June. The male elks roll in mud to keep insects off. The elk antlers are fully grown by August, and shed their velvet covering. Calves loose all their spots by fall.

---

[1] *Enterprise Mountaineer* Monday, February 5, 2001.

Elk are larger than the black bear in the Park; the males weigh 600 to 700 pounds. Cows usually about 500 pounds and stand 4½ to 5 ft. tall. Sometimes the antlers grow to five feet in width.

Elk mostly eat grasses, acorns, bark, buds, shrubs and leaves. Their predators are coyote, bobcats and black bears, may kill young sick or injured elk. Cows give birth once a year. Female elk are ready to breed by the second fall, when they are 2 years old.

Elk lifespan is about fifteen years. They have an acute sense of smell and excellent eyesight. These large animals can be very dangerous. Female elk with calves have charged people in defense of their off spring. Male (bulls) may perceive people as challengers to their domain and charge. It is best to keep your distance from them.

Feeding wildlife in the Park is strictly forbidden by law and can result in a very high fine.

In the wintertime the Park had a person to feed the elk hay and keep check on them.

January 2002 another herd of elk were put in Cataloochee. Some of the first herd roamed far and wide, they have been seen in White Oak, Jonathan Creek and Cherokee.

Now you can see them in Cataloochee Valley. They come out about sun up and at sundown.[1]

If all goes well the Park plans to bring in twenty-five more elk to Cataloochee in 2003.

An interesting story of the elk came from Kim Delozier head of the Elk Foundation in the Great Smoky Mountain National Park. They have collars on the elk and can tell where they go.

This particular cow was about ready to deliver her baby in June, she must have been scared by some of the several bears that were reported to be in Cataloochee at that time. Bears are the predators of the elk, especially the baby elk. They watch and wait for them to drop. This mama elk traveled all the way to the Cataloochee Balsam to have her baby, she stayed with it for some time, then she left it on the mountain (probably well hidden) she walked back down to the Valley, looked around real good, stayed a while. The bears must have left because she walked back up the mountain seven miles and brought her baby back down to the Valley. Think about it, she walked the seven miles up the mountain to have her baby, walked back down the seven miles to see if it was safe, then she walked back up the seven miles and brought her baby to the Valley which was a total of twenty eight miles, so you better believe

---

[1] *Enterprise Mountaineer 2002*

they will protect their offspring, and keep a long distance from them. This is just one example of how caring they really are.

Panther Seen in Cataloochee

There are some panthers stories in "*Reflections of Cataloochee*" we have no doubt but what they are true.

August 8, 1975 <u>The Waynesville Mountaineer</u> ran this story (in part). The panther an enormous cat which once roamed in large numbers throughout North America may have returned to its former home in Western North Carolina.

On July 23 at about 9 P.M. according to a report by four Great Smoky Mountain National Park maintenance men, a panther was seen chasing a deer in the Cataloochee Valley. Lee Cochran, Walter Law, Emmett Wiggins and Horace Cunningham all of Bryson City, had returned to the bunkhouse after a days work and were sitting on the porch after supper when the panther made its appearance.

"We saw a deer in a nearby field that looked like it was scared," Cochran said, "suddenly something darted across the field after the deer and crossed the road. Some other people saw it cross the road. We talked to the ranger, then discovered that two or three other people had heard something squall."

Upon further investigation, the Park employees discovered panther tracks beside the road where it had made its crossing and in some wet soil on the back side of the field. Cub tracks were discovered according to Cochran.

Gilbert W. Calhoun, acting superintendent, said this is the first confirmed sighting of a panther in the Park.

"The report was given to me by Cataloochee Ranger Tom Kaloos." Calhoun said, "The animal was described as being long tailed, and covered the ground in long leaps and bounds." Since that time there are numerous reports of sighting in Western North Carolina.

The cougars' main food is deer although it will feed on smaller animals. According to a book on North American mammals, a single bite by a mature cat at the base of the deer's skull will kill it.

An adult cat was reportedly seen on a road by a camper three weeks ago, and a maintenance foreman said he heard a scream at the Cataloochee overlook

Called by naturalist Bruce S. Wright as "the Ghost of North America" the panther is known by several names. The average length of a cougar (panther) is between six and eight feet and it weighs from 80 to 225 pounds. "Those animals can outrun a deer in a short burst." Calhoun said. "They range in color from tawny to gray, and are such shy animals that even trackers have trouble finding them."

"I've never heard one scream before, but people who have, say that once you do hear it, you'll never forget it."

Chapter 14

Short Stories

Crestmont, A Town on Mt. Sterling

In the early part of the 1900s some wealthy lumber companies found that there was lots of fine timber, some virgin timber growing in our mountains, the companies set up villages for their workers.

It is surprising today to find that Mt. Sterling had a large sawmill town, they named it Crestmont, which had two hotels, boarding houses, a club house, church, school, a movie theatre, a big commissary, a barber shop, a box factory, a sawmill and houses all on Mt. Sterling.

The Tennessee-North Carolina (T&NC) railroad, people called it the peavine. It took eight hours to make the twenty-one mile trip, climbing from Newport, Tennessee to Crestmont; somewhere around 6,000 ft. in elevation.

The train not only served as a lumber train, people from Little Cataloochee had hauled their apples and produce on wagons to Knoxville, Tennessee before the train. It was great to ship by train and sometimes when they needed to shop they would ride the train.

Some of the people in Big Cataloochee may have shipped by train but their elevation being 2680 ft. it would be very hard for the horses to pull a loaded wagon up the 6000+ ft. mountain.

The men from Big Cataloochee used to talk about going to Waynesville, N.C. with a loaded wagon. They would start very early in the morning and it took all day to get to the top of Cove Creek Mountain, where they would camp out for the night some would sleep on the ground with their head on their saddle or whatever they had. If it rained they slept under the wagon.

People from Big Cataloochee often rode a horse or a buggy up to Mt. Sterling to ride the train to Newport to shop.

My father, Eldridge Caldwell and Mother Pearl Valentine were taken up the mountain in a buggy, they went on the train to Newport, where they were married 1923. They went from there to Asheville, N.C. on their honeymoon.

After the fine timber was cut and hauled away the company dismantled the buildings and sold them in the late 40s. Now they say there are only a few traces left of the once thriving town of Crestmont, N.C.

There was lots of other logging areas such as Walnut Bottoms, Big Creek area, Round Bottom - above Cherokee, Smokemont - up above the Rangers Station at Oconaluftee, Ravensford - toward Big Cove out of Cherokee and probably several more.

These were large lumber operations it took the government several years to stop them. They were ruining all the small growth of trees, breaking everything over six ft. high, with overhead skidders, just cutting all the big timer, trimming off the limbs and brush, just leaving big heaps of brush everywhere. That was the main reason the Park was organized and finally got it stopped. That is why we have the Great Smoky Mountain National Park.

Of course it was a real heartbreak for most of the people who had to leave everything they had worked for, but today we have a big beautiful park, may we all be aware of its value and help take care of it.

Mt. Sterling

The story is that a man found a large thick vein of lead in the creek, he could chop out great chunks of it and make bullets, but at first he thought it to be sterling silver - because of its softness and grayish color. Then it was named Mt. Sterling.

Boogerman Trail

Caldwell Fork has several creeks. Thad Sutton said they had to cross the creek fifteen times from where he lived down to the valley. The North Carolina area of the Great Smoky Mountains and it contains 60,000 acres and there are many miles of trails in that area. Boogerman trail is one of them; people wonder how it got its name.

There was a timid little boy, his first day in school, the teacher asked each child to tell his name, he would not tell his name until all the other children did, the teacher asked him again. He said "Boogerman" and quickly put his head down on his arms on his desk, well he was called that the rest of his life, instead of Robert. He had a house in the area of Cataloochee Creek on the south side where the trail goes up Caldwell Fork of course it got the Boogerman name.

You can get maps of these trails from the Visitors Center in the Park and many local bookstores and outfitters sell them.

Caldwell Fork lies on the south side of Cataloochee Creek, no structures remain there now. There were several nice weather boarded houses and some beautiful log cabins, which would still be standing if only the roofs had been repaired or replaced.

After the people had to leave there nothing was done to preserve any of the buildings.

There never was a road up Caldwell Fork except a rough old wagon road with stumps, big rocks and deeply cut ruts. Only wagons had wheels high enough to get over the obstacles. Those who lived there had dug out, cut trees, and carried rock off to make the wagon road they worked very hard.

After the Park took over they built a narrow road up Caldwell Fork, so the ranger could go in a jeep to keep check on it.

No Fence Law

Farming in the early range days there were no stock law, which meant all livestock had free range. Farmers must build a fence of some sort to keep the cattle, hogs and sheep out of his crops and garden.

When the land was cleared of trees and stumps, then the rocks were carried or hauled on a sled to build a fence. There were many of the rock fences in Cataloochee.

Photo courtesy of: GSMNP

Rock removed from the field to make plowing and hoeing easier, rocks make a good strong fence.

When the Park took over, the roads were rough and rocky so they took the fences down and crushed the rocks to use for gravel on the roads.

Rail fence were usually 8 to 10 rails high built of chestnut or locust.
Photo courtesy of: GSMNP

Post and rider fence, most likely built of chestnut rails.
Photo courtesy of: GSMNP

At that time there were lots of rail fences, but they disassembled them because it was suppose to turn back into a wilderness of the Great Smoky Mountains.

Later when those first Park officials retired or died, then young people were hired. Thank goodness they recognize the value of the history and are helping to restore and keep as much as possible.

Since the "Friends of the Smokies" was organized they have been able to get some great contributions, but still need more. Let us all make tax-free contributions to them, to help keep the small portion we have left.

Cemeteries

All the cemeteries are on top of steep hills. Many people have inquired how could they get a body up the steep hill for burial?

The trails that go straight up the hills have been made by visitors to the Park, not by the natives who lived there.

The casket was placed on a sled then taken down the road, then a road turned toward the cemetery at an angle gradually going up hill until they reached the top.

Photo courtesy of Louise Nelson

Diseases and Remedies

In the early 1900's there were several dreaded diseases: T.B. (Tuberculosis) typhoid fever were very bad, many died. Some died from ruptured appendix but the worst of all was the influenza epidemic, which started about 1918. It killed over 20 million people worldwide.

I have heard of one man going to see about his neighbor, when he got there he found 5 had died in the floor in front of the fireplace. It was just a horrible time; some families lost 3 or 4 in one week. They were not able to bury them as fast as they died. They knew the disease was very contagious. In order to save the rest of the family, some were buried without a casket; by the time they got back to the house another one had died.

The influenza was especially hard on infants and small children and took a high toll. If you visit cemeteries and find little graves marked only by fieldstones, it may have been some of those children because many died.

In 1911 there was an outbreak of smallpox and many fell victim of it, but the death toll was not nearly as high as the influenza, which swept the world. One woman had six children, they all died in 3 weeks, her husband off fighting in WWI.

There was not much medicine in those years like we have today, and doctors were few and far between his office and his patients.

Some of the doctors were self taught and very dedicated. Many people used their home remedies that had been handed down through the years. Roots and herbs were gathered and used to prepare the home remedies. Herbs and roots were such as catnip, boneset, sage, basil, penny rile, horsemint, snakeroot, ferns, pepper and others. Kerosene was poured on a cut, sometimes kerosene and coal soot were used for big cuts. Whiskey, ginger and honey were used to soothe a cold.

Many of those home remedies worked very well and were used by the early doctors for his patients. Lots of those home remedies were learned from the Indians. We wish we knew more of those tried and true remedies today.[1]

---

[1] From Helen and Junior Ball ***History of Mt. Sterling, N.C.*** in part.

White Swelling

Several people have told me about grandpa Hiram Caldwell, they say he was a jokey old fellow, always joking and laughing. He raised cattle and hogs for his income.

Of course they always had a smokehouse full of cured hams. They used brown sugar, salt and pepper to cure the hams and they were delicious, we always had hot biscuits and gravy with the fried ham along with lots of other good food.

Grandpa, his brother Harrison and John all three got swollen legs and feet in their later years. Their legs swelled more than twice their normal size, in some cases the skin would burst.

Sometimes they called it heart dropsy. They couldn't walk far until they had to sit. In later stages they had to sit with their feet and legs elevated. They all died of heart trouble.

Today we know salt causes fluid retention in the body, but I suppose they did not realize that salty ham was probably the cause of their illness.

Bee Burgess Palmer Sisk said she and her mother walked from Little Cataloochee, about five miles, to see grandpa, he was setting up with his feet up in another chair, he died a short while later at age of 71.

Smoke Chaser

Homer Caldwell, son of Uncle George, married Flora Burress, they had 1 son, Marshall and 1 daughter Juanita. Homer was not very strong due to asthma. They had a big farm one mile up Shanty Branch.

Homer got a job with the Forest Service; his job was to travel to some of the highest peaks to keep a look out for forest fires.

He rode his horse and had to make a report of where he traveled to and how many miles. Here are some copies of some of his reports:

May 7, 1934 leaving home at 9:00 o'clock am. Patrol out to head of Palmer Creek up lead to Tote Rock back to Pin Oak. Returned to camp at 7 o'clock

Hours 10 Miles 12

May 9, 1934

Left home at 7:00 am patrol up lead to Balsam Top. Returned to camp at 6:00 pm 11 hours 10 miles

April 27, 1934

Left home at 8: am patrol out to Trail Ridge, began snowing and raining

Returned home 3 hours 4 miles

April 28, 1934

Left home at 7:am patrol Pin Oak Gap out Main Lead to Ledge Ball on the Beach Gap around Riser's Creek Grade a ways. Return home 6 pm 11 hours 15 miles

(April 29, 1934 snowing again)

Homer must not have been feeling very well one had, he wrote a note in the back of his notebook: If found dead put me away at the grave yard where my dad is: Homer Caldwell

Nellie, N.C. (name of Post office in Cataloochee

Forest Service Warden, Straight Fork District.

Another note: April, 8,9 and 10 rain

April 12, 1934 Snowing

April 13, 1934 snow on the ground

This information comes from Homer's grandson Erick, who has the original notebook. This is just a few of the many pages. He had to write a report for each day.

Covered Wagon

In an interview January 2002, with Mrs. Otis (Noland) Burgin now 97 years of age told of her family living at Fines Creek and how they would gather up their things and load up the covered wagon and come over to Cataloochee and camp out for a week at a time, this was 1923-1924. They were friends of the William Palmer family and camped in the field below the Post office (below Palmer Church). She said they would fish and cook out just have a good ol' time. She still remembered the rough rocky muddy roads cut deep by the steel rim wagon wheels.

Mrs. Burgin said sometimes they would go to Dallas Clark's place at Fines Creek and walk the early trail to the mouth of Cataloochee Creek and camp there later on the tunnel was dug and all the water was channeled into it and about 7 miles to the Waterville Dam.

She said her daddy was the first to buy a car on Fines Creek, it was a 1914 or 1915 Ford, and that horses were scarred of it and would run away when one came near. Some people never had seen a car were afraid of the car too, some running and climbing up in a tree or anywhere they thought that thing couldn't get them.

Kerr Place

The Kerrs (pronounced Carr) had a lodge on the road in the direction of Mount Stirling; sometimes in the early years they kept tourist, fishermen and hunters. Older people say the Kerrs had some slaves working for them, and when the slaves died, they were buried somewhere near the Kerr place. They say there are three rocks used as headstones. Some think there may have been as many as ten slaves buried there, but there were always plenty of rocks, seems like if there were more graves there would be more rock markers.

The oldest people I have talked to say they never saw any slaves only heard the story. After the Civil War the Kerrs told the slaves they were free to go, but they said no, they wanted to stay because they had been treated well that was home to them. (Source: R.C. Sutton – born Caldwell Fork)

Kerrs had bought the slaves to grow cotton, but the land was not suitable. They grew most of the food necessary to feed their guests. These were the only black people ever to live in Cataloochee.

Cataloochee Township

This township had six thriving communities before it was taken over for the Great Smoky Mountain National Park.

I have written about the three communities, Big Cataloochee, Little Cataloochee and Caldwell Fork all of which lie over Cove Creek Mountain 4,600 ft. high. In order to get to the other three communities, Big Creek, Big Bend and Mt. Sterling which is over 6,000 feet high you could reach it by traveling up Cosby Tennessee road or go over Cove Creek then up over Mt Sterling

Junior and Helen Bald have written two books about the History of Mt. Sterling and its people this also includes Big Creek and Big Bend. They have listed many cemeteries in the area and much information from the headstones giving birth and death dates.

They have also given some genealogy of Sparks, Miller, Barnes, Ball, Baxter, Browns, Moore, Naillon, Price, Sutton, Phillips, Gates, Messer, Noland, Palmer, McGee, Leatherwood, Lockman, Hicks, McGaha, Grooms, Hopkins and the names of their spouses.

There are lots of photographs and information in their books.

Junior and Helen Ball
654 Hale Brook Rd.
Newport, TN 37821

Christy

You most likely have seen the movie Christy; it's a good movie. A story of a young schoolteacher from Asheville, N.C. who went to the mountains of Tennessee to teach at a Presbyterian mission. As I remember she found about 100 starving children being taken care of, fed and taught at the mission school. In the movie several times one of the main actors would look out across the mountain and say I wonder how things are in Cataloochee, but the school was no where near Cataloochee. It was in Del Rio, Tenn. Down the other side of Mount Sterling, in Cock Co. Tenn.

Moonshine

A Judge was trying a fellow for making whiskey. The Judge said, "Now, I have heard that whiskey is better after it has been kept awhile and aged, is that true? The man spake up, "Your Honor, you have been misinformed. I kept some liquor a whole week one time and it was no better than when it was new and fresh. (*Random Thoughts and Musings of a Mountaineer* - Judge Felix Alley)

Aunt Susie

Aunt Susie Woody Caldwell (photo page 80 in *Reflections of Cataloochee*) was a midwife, she must have delivered babies most of her life, because she delivered me, my mother said she was very good at it. I subtracted my (this writers) birth date from her birth date and discovered she was 77 years old at that time she delivered me.

Page 81 in *Reflections of Cataloochee* is photo of Hiram and Mary Elizabeth Howell Caldwell who had the Caldwell House built. They started building 1898 finished 1903 - five years to build because there was no electricity, definitely hand built and besides the cattle and other livestock and farming had to be taken care of.

SIDE SADDLE

Grandma Caldwell's sidesaddle

Grandpa Hiram Caldwell had this sidesaddle made special for grandma (Mary Elizabeth Howell Caldwell) in 1898 by the Pickett Brothers in Asheville, N.C.

In those days it was proper for ladies to ride sidesaddle, they sat in the saddle with both legs over to the side, they wore long dress, there were not supposed to show their ankles. The curved horn held the legs. There was a stirrup to mount up with.

Daddy told me a story about this saddle, when he was just two or three years old, grandma was riding in this saddle and had him on her lap, they went to visit a neighbor and on the way home some yellow jackets got under the saddle and stung the horse, which bucked and jumped, throwing them to the ground. He said his Mother was really hurt bad, bruised and cut on rocks, but never the less she kept him cradled in her arms and he was not hurt at all. That saddle had a very special meaning to him.

This bonnet was grandmas Sunday bonnet. She always made two extra; for working in the garden, when one got dirty she would wash it then always have a clean one to wear.

Her Sunday bonnet was always black taffeta or satin, she made all of her clothes, and her Sunday dress was always black. She made her everyday dresses and bonnets of tiny checked gingham either navy and white, or black and white checks. She always made matching aprons, almost as long as her dresses. All her dresses buttoned up to the neck, had long sleeves and long skirts all the way to her shoes. That was customary of how the women of her time dressed (see pages 192 and 193 in *Reflections of Cataloochee*) and I never heard of any of them getting skin cancer.

Aunt Mag Mooney Caldwell

Aunt Mag

Aunt Mag Mooney (also spelled Mauney) Caldwell, born 1858 wife of George Henry Caldwell loved to smoke her corn cob pipe but she only smoked it after lunch or dinner. She always sat in front of the fireplace so the smoke would go up the chimney. Several of the women used snuff and a few smoked their pipe - that was their only vise.

Those dear old Cataloochee people missed each other so much after having to leave Cataloochee, having to move to various locations, most of the older ones were homesick and longing for the company of their dear old friends. When they got the opportunity to come and visit they would stay a week or so.

Aunt Mag came to visit and us kids thought it was great to see her smoke. Her grandson Raymond Caldwell said he had rode in her buggy with her and corncob pipe had a stem made of cane. He said they buried her on Christmas day 1949. At that time she had four large canisters of Prince Albert tobacco, people knew she liked to smoke and that people had given it to her for Christmas.

Their Spirit Didn't Leave

Now the Cataloochee people are gone from their beloved homeland gone, long gone, most have been gone for more than sixty-eight years (since 1934).

Yes they are all gone from there but their spirit is still there, it refused to leave, it welcomes you as in yesteryear. You can feel it floating around in the fields and the hills and along the creek as it is swiftly flowing by. The houses and barns are haunted by their spirit.

Stop and listen, meditate for a while, you may feel a presence like a sudden light breeze something is almost touching you in this glorious place. Their spirit seems strongest in the churches and cemeteries.

Their friendly spirit will always be there to welcome you and extend their hospitality to who ever comes here. Perhaps that is the reason you get that calm and relaxed feeling when you are there.

The people had to leave their beautiful special place but their spirits refused to go, they stayed on to watch over the homeland it is like hallowed ground.

When our people go back for their reunion, something is restored in them as they attend church, pray and sing the old hymns then hug each other and renew old acquaintances.

We stand by the cool clear rushing creeks, smell the spicy clean fragrance of the pines and watch the beautiful tall ferns gently waving in the breeze as we reminisce our pleasant memories of long ago.

We continue with a long walk just to drink in all the beauty that God has created for us, it is overwhelming; it's majestic beauty and splendor. But my heart aches in memory of those pioneers who had a hard struggle to get a start and eventually saw their dreams come true and they lived well and then have to loose it all.

Now it is gone all gone never to return to the peaceful happy place our ancestors once knew. It is haunted by the friendly spirit of the long ago people of Cataloochee. The place has a spirit, a soul, its very mystical, we can't just let the wonderful legacy die, for someday we will be gone, but my sincere hope is that our roots run deep enough and there is enough loyalty in our younger generations to continue this pilgrimage in honor of our grand ancestors.

It is my prayer that our descendants will convey this wonderful heritage to their young, that each generation will take pride in their heritage and come to the little churches to think and pray, to get in touch with God and nature and to pay homage to our ancestors who so richly deserve it.

Pearl Throws Hat Away

Hub Caldwell had carried the mail by horse and buggy, and then got an early Model Ford, he was driving to Waynesville. My daddy and Mother (Eldridge and Pearl Caldwell) were riding to Waynesville with him one day. As they were going up the steep mountain, the gravity flow of gas was much like Mr. Barbers. They got way up the mountain and all of a sudden the car starts going backward down the step, narrow, crooked road. My mother was sitting beside of Hub, she was scared and so excited, she reached over and snatched his hat off and sailed it out the window. It happened so quick, daddy said he couldn't do a thing except watch it sail out over the treetops and many feet below, straight down!

Well Hub was busy backing down the road and around the curves at a faster speed than he wanted, but finally he saw a soft bank of dirt he backed into it, getting it stopped.

Hub was hoppin' mad about his hat and said daddy had to go get it, daddy offered to buy him a hat just as soon as they got to town, but Hub said no, it is my fine Panama straw hat and I ordered it, they don't have them in Waynesville.

Daddy knew that Hub always wore a white hat and had much pride in how he looked in public as most of the Cataloochee people did. Working on the farm they did not worry about their looks, but for now he had to get down the side of that steep mountain and try to find Hub's hat. He said, heck it was hard to keep from falling down the mountain, then took quite a while to find it then getting back up was harder, he just had to pull up by bushes and practically crawl up that steep mountain, he was mad about the hard trip, but he was too nice and too gentle to say much. Mother said she apologized to Hub; she had no idea why she did such a foolish thing. The last we talked about it was in the 70s. I think Daddy was still mad! But he would just grin and Mother would laugh and say, I don't know why I did that.

I think it was her first trip across the mountain in a car.

5 Million Dollar Donation

Even before 1900 there were requests for a National Park in the south. Finally by 1927 North Carolina General assembly passed a bill for a state bond issue in the amount of two million dollars to buy the land for a Park, but that was not near enough. Several people made pledges to help pay for it. Tennessee would contribute the same amount as North Carolina, but they were still short. The estimated cost was ten million dollars, then John D. Rockefeller Jr. donated five million to complete the amount needed to buy the land, homes and all. The five million dollars was a memorial to his mother Laura Spellman Rockefeller.

The Park was dedicated in 1940 by President Franklin D. Roosevelt at Clingman's Dome; he had one foot in Tennessee and one in North Carolina.

A bronze plaque was erected there at Clingman's Dome as a memorial to Laura Spellman Rockefeller.

With all of this writing of the history of Cataloochee (two books and a tour guide) can provide material for an in-depth study of a mountain community, a first rate social and economic history of the three close knit areas which were practically isolated from the rest of the world for more than 100 years.

This history is written to preserve and pass on to future generations of a heritage and an experience worth preserving and passing on, and to be a source of pride for Cataloochans and their descendants.

About the Author

Hattie Caldwell Davis, was the third and last generation born in Cataloochee, her family and most all of the people had been living and working there since 1834, some more than one hundred years.

As the years went by, more and more of the older generation were dying. This author could see those dear old folks who had lived the history would soon be gone and the history would die with them, she began doing interviews, collecting all the information and photos that she could get, she saved articles from newspapers about Cataloochee natives and is grateful for these articles, photos and information given to her by the Cataloochee people and the newspapers for they all helped to preserve this history. Dr. Carroll's research is priceless, for without it this history would never have been as complete as we now have it.

It is by no means complete, but enough information has been gathered to show that we had ancestors worthy of any and all honor we can bestow upon them.

This author felt that we owe our ancestors a debt of gratitude and in some small way this helps to pay the debt to them and to inform the descendants of their fine heritage.

Writing this book has been a labor of love, now I leave you this great legacy.

Hattie Caldwell Davis

Corrections for *Reflections of Cataloochee:*

Page 220 has a photo of Claude Caldwell And family child sitting on his lap is daughter Lola Caldwell (Rolland) **not** Hazel as listed she was born later. Evelyn gave me the photo, she said they all had had shots for smallpox, they were not in the mood to sit and wait for the photograph to be made.

Correction:

Page 281 photo of Aunt Mag (b. 1-11-1858) holding her son Roscoe - Born 1882 photo taken maybe a year or more later - notice his high round neck garment, looks like Old English style of the 1600s.

Bibliography

This continued history of Cataloochee has been condensed from the research material of:

Doctor Roy Carroll's Historic Structures Report.

Historian Edward Trout's Historic Structures Report - Big Cataloochee.

Mr. Clark Medford's Early History of Haywood Co.

Mr. Hiram Wilburn's notes of Cataloochee People in the 20s and 30s.

Speeches made at our reunion by:

Dr. H. Woody - History Professor at Duke

Dr. Myron L. Coulter - Chancellor at Western Carolina University.

Congressman Lamar Gudger - US House of Representatives.

Dr. Roy Carroll - Appalachian State University 1976.

Articles from:

The Enterprise Mountaineer

The Asheville Citizen Times

GSMNP Archives for many photographs

Judge Felix Alley - *Random Thoughts and Musings of a Mountaineer*

Acknowledgments

The author wishes to express our most sincere appreciation to Dr. Roy Carroll, Raymond H. Pulley and their crew of dedicated people who helped to collect the history and facts for the Historic Structures Report for the Great Smoky Mountain National Park 1976 and all the Park personnel who helped make the study possible, especially Edward L. Trout, who was Park Historian. He had a real appreciation of history and put all of his effort into getting the project done, to save as much history as possible. It is great to have all the facts researched so thoroughly; we owe them a debt of gratitude for all their help. (See page 297 in *Reflections of Cataloochee)*

We are grateful to have all of this information to combine with other research information and photos we have collected.

We thank Beatrice Burgess Palmer Sisk for writing about growing up in Little Cataloochee.

Dr. Carroll said, our aim in this is quite simple - to preserve and pass on to future generations a heritage and an experience worth preserving and passing on. We want our study of the community to be a source of pride for Cataloochans and the descendants and you are right, your generation, the third and last generation to be born there, has a genuine concern and a great responsibility to see that it is done.

Many thanks to Eunave Palmer Perkins for copies of letters from Burdine Childress, for information about the Cook's trip to California also Joyce Cook Reeves for photos and information. We are grateful to Wilson Medford for permission to write about the Cataloochee

Turnpike and cattle drives from his father Mr. W.C. Medford's *Early History of Haywood Co.*

It was really a treat to get our Naillon genealogy, many thanks to Jean Wiggleworth of Ohio, who sent it, after reading *"Reflections of Cataloochee."* We knew very little about Granny Pop's family (Mary Ann Naillon Colwell) she was just about everybody's grandmother, many, many can trace their roots back to her and back to Ireland. Additional photos and Naillon information were sent from Junior and Helen Ball, many thanks to them. We appreciate the story Eric Caldwell gave about his grandfather Homer Caldwell - A Smoke Chaser. Thanks to Mrs. Otis Burgin for her story of going to Cataloochee in a covered wagon. It is great that Vernon Palmer is 100 years of age and could very well remember carrying the mail by horse and buggy from Cataloochee to Cove Creek and he attended the reunion last August (2002). Mr. Richard N. Barber gave us a wonderful story of going to Cataloochee in 1918 or 1919. We treasure his stories, he is now deceased, he will be missed at our reunions. We thank R.C. Sutton for information about the Kerr Place (Carr).

We are grateful to Mary Woody Dunn and her sister Alice Woody Shook for information and photographs. Many thanks to Mildred Hannah Hazel of Fairfax, Va. who gave us a great photograph and names of school children about 1908 at Little Cataloochee school.

Our thanks to Louise Brooks Snyder (a descendant of William R. Noland of Cataloochee) who gave us a great story and photographs to prove it.

We extend our thanks and appreciation to all who have sent us photos:

Wade Caldwell
Scott Sutton
Gudger Palmer
Douglas Smathers
Linda Fulbright Rathbone
Forence and Ethan Evans
Roger Ford
Gilmer Caldwell
Cora Moody Caldwell
Chris Cirrincione
Gary Stamey

And to anyone that I failed to record their names. Thanks to those who sent us photographs of the elk.

Dave Kaushik, Five Points, TN.
Fred Weiser, Townsend TN.
George Stitz, Ohio
Hershel Caldwell, Waynesville

We appreciate Hershel Caldwell and all who help him get the picnic tables out, clean them off and set them out for us at reunion time. And we certainly appreciate them cleaning the church and dusting the benches for our church service. Hershel is a volunteer who helps clear the trails and does other jobs for the Park.

We thank Steve Woody for being our Master of Ceremonies. Also Linton Palmer, Raymond Caldwell and others who help to organize our reunion. We thank Raymond and Jackie Caldwell for keeping records of all of our Cataloochee people who have deceased each year.

Thanks to Louise Palmer Ross who is secretary/treasure and keeps our records.

We appreciate all the work the Park Service does, mowing the grass, setting up port-a-potties and help direct traffic. Everyone works together to make it nice.